Slow Cooker 2

100 brand new recipes from the author of *Slow Cooker*

SALLY WISE

ABC
Books

*This book is dedicated to my husband and
children and to all those who share a love of slow-cooking.*

The ABC 'Wave' device is a trademark of the
Australian Broadcasting Corporation and is used
under licence by HarperCollins*Publishers* Australia.

First published in Australia in 2012
by HarperCollins*Publishers* Australia Pty Limited
ABN 36 009 913 517
harpercollins.com.au

Text copyright © Sally Wise 2012

HarperCollins*Publishers*
Level 13, 201 Elizabeth Street, Sydney NSW 2000, Australia
Unit D, 63 Apollo Drive, Rosedale, Auckland 0632, New Zealand
A 53, Sector 57, Noida, UP, India
1 London Bridge Street, London SE1 9GF, United Kingdom
2 Bloor Street East, 20th floor, Toronto, Ontario M4W 1A8, Canada
195 Broadway NY, NY 10007, United States of America

National Library of Australia Cataloguing-in-Publication data:

Wise, Sally.
  Slow cooker 2 : 100 brand new recipes
  Sally Wise.
  ISBN 978 0 7333 3103 9 (pbk.)
  Electric cooking, slow.
  Casserole cooking.
641.5884

Cover design by Matt Stanton, HarperCollins Design Studio
Cover photograph by Stuart Scott
Typeset in 11.5/15pt Centaur MT by Kirby Jones
Printed and bound in Australia by Griffin Press
The papers used by HarperCollins in the manufacture of this book are a natural, recyclable product
made from wood grown in sustainable plantation forests. The fibre source and manufacturing
processes meet recognised international environmental standards, and carry certification.

Contents

Acknowledgements

Thanks to my wonderful family who share a passion for food and cooking and a love for working with seasonal produce.

Special thanks to ABC presenter Chris Wisbey for his ongoing encouragement and support.

Much appreciation goes to the people who visit our house and become test tasting conscripts.

Thanks to Bev and Phil from Doolishus Food Van at Eaglehawk Neck for their generous help in providing the best quality fresh fish for developing the seafood recipes in this book. Thanks also to Pauline O'Carolan.

To the exceptional team at ABC Books/HarperCollins who do such a great job in the publishing and promotion of my books – with special thanks to Amruta Slee, Karen Penning, Julia Collingwood, Julie Bullock, Helen Biles, Matt Stanton and Nicola Wood.

INTRODUCTION

Slow-cooking has been used and valued for centuries due to the magnificent flavours resulting from the long, slow, cooking process; as well, there is the convenience for families, business people, young people – for anyone, in fact, who likes to have cooking simplified without sacrificing nutritional value and flavour.

I recently read an account of how in times past farmers working in fields made good use of a form of slow-cooking. Rather than the farm workers returning to the homestead for lunch, early in the morning their wives would prepare a casserole-style dish and heat it till well boiling. It would be turned out into a clay dish with a lid and placed in an old biscuit tin, which, at that time, could be readily acquired from grocers who purchased bulk biscuits in tins. The casserole dish was then packed tightly all around with straw to keep the heat in and slow cook the food. The men would take this out with them and by midday the hot casserole would be cooked to perfection.

Slow cookers are amazingly adaptable. They are wonderful for having a hot meal to come home to after work or recreation. Even on a day at home, I find it's so good to put something in the slow cooker early, leaving the rest of the day free in the sure knowledge that dinner is organised. I admit to being a messy cook, so it also allows time for a clean-up. A dinner can be started hours in advance so that by mealtime, all you need to do is serve.

When I was asked to write a second slow cooker book, I thought it would be a tall order. However, I have thoroughly enjoyed the process – experimenting further, exploring different flavours and methods of cooking with my (remaining six) slow cookers. I'm afraid a few slow cookers have been casualties along the way – through overwork, I strongly suspect. A friend recently remarked that our yard is a slow-

I

cooker graveyard. All the clay inserts from every slow cooker that I've worn out now serve as drinking vessels for the dog, chooks, ducks and wildlife. They're very practical as the water stays cool even in hot weather – the insert keeps it that way.

In this book, only one of the recipes (Steak and Kidney Pudding – page 176) calls for browning of the meat. Of course you can brown the meat in the other recipes if you want, but it is another step you can do without when you are in a hurry. The ingredients are carefully balanced to make sure that there is plenty of flavour.

A healthy breakfast is easy – you can cook porridge, a fruit compote or rancher's eggs overnight, ready to serve as soon as you get up. I wondered for a long time how to accomplish the porridge factor – it always turned to stodge using regular rolled oats; however, if you use steel cut oats, available from health food stores, the porridge is perfect – and is also very economical and healthy.

Cleaning the slow cooker is a dream. I simply pour about 8 centimetres of hot water in the still-warm empty cooker, leave it with the lid on for about 30 minutes and it can be wiped clean with no scrubbing.

I gave away one of my slow cookers after writing the first slow cooker book, thinking to keep five was excessive. Eventually I went and bought a replacement for it. I can do a meal for many so very easily – a soup in one, a meat dish in another, vegetable dishes in another two and a dessert in the fifth. I like having a range of sizes, depending on the number I'm serving, but if I had to choose the most versatile size, it would be an oval 3.5 litre capacity, which is ideal for a family of four and is large enough to hold a roast. If you have a smaller family, then leftovers can be refrigerated or frozen for another day.

For single people or small families, it is a good idea to seek out a smaller cooker – a 1.5 litre is available through some of the larger retail outlets. This capacity serves two or three people. I have two of these, and an old

1970s Monier I litre capacity, all of which are very handy to make porridge, savoury dishes or smaller desserts.

Perhaps the best aspect of using a slow cooker is that it reduces the temptation to buy take-away on the way home. This is not only better for the budget, but you know what is in the meal, thus sparing yourself all the additives that may well be hidden in commercially prepared products.

I like to think of using a slow cooker as a form of slow fast cooking. It is fast in the preparation of placing ingredients in the cooker; it cooks slowly without fuss and attention, then is fast and easy to serve at mealtimes.

So, whatever your family size, whatever your lifestyle or circumstance, there is always a place for at least one slow cooker to make your life so much easier.

GENERAL

HELPFUL

HINTS

Many slow cookers have two or more temperature settings. These settings can vary from one cooker to the next, so it is very important to read the manufacturer's instructions carefully.

Most modern cookers have a 'Low' and a 'High' setting. Some will have an 'Auto' option, which means it starts cooking at High, then switches automatically to Low. If a cooker has a 'Keep Warm' setting, it means that after the food is cooked it will hold the food at a safe temperature until serving time. Some cookers have timers, which cook the food for a specified time, then switch automatically to 'Keep Warm' until serving time. Some have the option to brown the meat in a removable insert, before returning it to the cooker to complete cooking.

When purchasing a slow cooker and wondering about the right size for your needs, think about what you will be using the cooker for. A small family? Entertaining? Is one enough? Also consider if you want one with a round or oval shape – the latter is better for cooking certain roasts, such as a leg of lamb.

Most of the recipes in this book serve four to six people. The recommended capacity of the slow cooker is indicated at the beginning of each recipe. To feed more, use a larger cooker and increase the quantities of ingredients correspondingly. Keep in mind that the cooker should not be filled to more than 3 centimetres from the top.

A very handy size is the smaller 1.5 litre capacity cooker (serves two to three people). I find that the food tends to cook in a shorter amount of time so if I'm going out I use the Low setting. If using this smaller cooker, reduce the quantities of ingredients correspondingly in the recipe.

Is Slow-cooking Safe?

Yes, slow cookers cook foods at a lower temperature for an extended period of time, but the temperatures reach a level far above the recommended food safety levels. Any bacteria are destroyed by the multi-directional heat combined with the steam created in the tightly sealed container.

Times and Temperatures

The amount of time dishes take to cook can vary, so always allow plenty of time. It is highly unlikely that the food will overcook, especially on Low. Even on High an extra hour will have no detrimental effect. I've cooked some meals for several hours extra on Low with no ill effect. The meat and vegetables were still intact and the meat delightfully tender.

As a general rule, the Low setting is approximately 94°C (200°F) and the High setting is approximately 149°C (300°F).

One hour on High is more or less equivalent to 2 hours on Low. This may vary to a degree in some recipes, which will have instructions to this effect. Some recipes require cooking on a specific setting. For meat dishes, as a general guide only, you can use the following table. Check for information in the instruction book for your cooker for any variations.

Conventional recipe times	Slow Cooker – Low	Slow Cooker – High
15 to 30 minutes	4 to 7 hours	1½ to 2½ hours
35 to 50 minutes	6 to 9 hours	3 to 4 hours
50 minutes to 3 hours	8 to 16 hours	4 to 6 hours

Note: *Recipes can be cooked for 1–2 hours on High and then reduced to Low if this is convenient.*

For Safety's Sake

If the power goes off when you are not at home, you will unfortunately need to discard the food because the temperature may have dropped to unsafe levels, causing the food to spoil.

If you have an old cooker, you can quite easily test to see if it is cooking to temperature. Fill the cooker with about 2 litres of cool water (less of course for a smaller cooker), cover with the lid, then heat on Low for 8 hours. Remove the lid and immediately check the temperature with a food thermometer. The temperature should be about 85°C (185°F). If the temperature is lower, the cooker may not be heating effectively enough to be safe.

Always defrost foods before adding them to the slow cooker. And certainly don't use the slow cooker to defrost foods.

If you wish to prepare foods the night before to set on to cook the next morning, it is best not to put the prepared ingredients into the cooker insert and then refrigerate it overnight. This is because the chilled insert takes longer to come up to the required temperature in the cooker. Instead, store the ingredients in containers in the fridge (keep meat and vegetables separate). It only takes a few moments to combine them in the cooker the next day. Make sure also to wipe away any food on the rim of the cooker insert after preparing ingredients in the cooker, so that a good seal forms with the lid during cooking.

When cooking foods in the cooker at altitudes over 1067 metres above sea level, you will need to extend the recommended cooking time by 50 per cent.

According to food experts, food should not be reheated in the slow cooker.

It is best not to leave leftovers in the cooker as they take a long time to cool down, meaning that bacteria could potentially grow in the food during this time. Instead, place them in containers and store in the fridge or freezer. Leftovers are very tasty indeed the next day and make wonderful fillings for pies. Leftovers can usually be frozen for up to 3 months.

Some people recommend using an external timer for the cooker. This means that the food is placed in the cooker and set to turn on at a specific time if anyone is away from the house. Although this may be very convenient, it does carry significant risks – for instance, the food left standing at room temperature may develop harmful bacteria. As a general rule, don't leave food waiting to be cooked at room temperature.

General Tips

Preheating on High may be recommended for your brand of slow cooker. Follow the manufacturer's directions in the instruction manual that comes with your cooker. If someone has donated a cooker to you minus the accompanying manual, it would be best to preheat for 15 minutes.

Always make sure not to overfill the cooker – no more than halfway to two-thirds full – otherwise the seal may not form effectively.

When lifting the lid from your cooker, lift straight up and away from the cooker so that the moisture on the lid doesn't fall back into the food.

Oven bags can be used to line the slow cooker insert, which will reduce washing up, although some instruction manuals carry a warning that they should not be used with chicken, lamb, pork or beef.

Some slow cooker inserts can be placed in the oven preheated to 160°C to brown toppings etc at the end of the cooking time. Check the manufacturer's manual to be sure.

Slow cookers don't like fat, so cut visible fat and skin from meat and poultry before adding to the cooker.

Generally it is not necessary to stir during cooking time, so don't be tempted to lift the lid unless it is to add dumplings or toppings, soft or thawed frozen vegetables, or dairy in the latter stages of cooking. Each time the lid is lifted, an extra 20–30 minutes must be added onto the cooking time. This is because the steam that results from slow-cooking creates a seal with the lid, and when the lid is lifted this seal is broken and needs to form again. Heat is also lost each time the lid is lifted.

If the dish is not cooked, replace the lid, set the cooker to High and cook in 30-minute increments. Always allow plenty of time.

Don't place the hot slow cooker insert on a cold surface, nor a very cold slow cooker insert into a hot unit.

Don't pour cold water into a hot slow cooker or hot water into a cold slow cooker.

Liquid Content

Use about half the recommended amount as you would in a conventional recipe, unless otherwise stated. One cup of liquid for a casserole-style dish is generally more than ample. If you find that the dish has too much liquid for your liking, simply turn the setting to High during the last hour of cooking. Some books recommend taking off the lid and turning the cooker to High for a time, to reduce the excess liquid, but I've not always found this to be successful as heat is lost. It is more successful if the lid is placed back on the slow cooker. Often, I instead take out most of the excess liquid with a soup ladle and put it into a small saucepan. I cook it over high heat on the stovetop until it reduces right down, and then return it to the slow cooker. It only takes a few minutes and needs little attention. In this way the flavours are retained and intensified.

Another trick is to thicken the sauce in the saucepan with cornflour paste (up to 1 tablespoon of cornflour mixed to a paste with a little cold water), stirring constantly while adding, and using only as much as is needed to thicken to the desired consistency. Then return the resulting gravy to the cooker. Cook on High for a few minutes more.

Many casseroles can be thickened in the cooker itself quite effectively (particularly on the High setting) by merely stirring in some cornflour paste, as the density and heat of the food is enough to induce the thickening in conjunction with the cornflour.

The Flavour Factor

It is sometimes claimed that during long slow-cooking some of the flavours of the food are diminished. In fact, I have rarely found this to be the case, but I have a range of simple products on stand-by as flavour enhancers, should they ever be necessary. It is really important to taste the food before serving (as with any form of cooking), so that flavours can be adjusted if necessary.

Although I generally refrain from using anything reeking of artificiality, I do keep on hand top-quality beef, vegetable and chicken stock powders.

The other items on the list of (good-quality) flavourings include:

soy sauce
Worcestershire sauce
sweet chilli sauce
barbecue sauce
fish sauce
chutney or relish

tomato sauce (ketchup)
quince or redcurrant jelly
raspberry jam
marmalade
apricot jam
honey

You can use the commercial product or make your own (except for the soy sauce) – there are many easy recipes in my book *A Year in a Bottle*.

Soups

Only add enough water to barely cover the ingredients and add extra water later if necessary. To make a cream soup, I make a cheese or cream sauce on the stovetop and add this at the end. This sauce can be made any time and reheated before adding to the slow cooker. Another method is to add cream or evaporated milk at the end of cooking time, replacing the lid on the cooker, turning the setting to High and reheating for approximately 20 minutes.

For a really rich soup, a combination of cream and egg yolks can be stirred in at the end of cooking time. This is indicated in specific recipes in this book.

Rice and Pasta

The same amount of water can be used as for conventional cooking, or reduce by one-third at most.

Rice and pasta should never be cooked for an extended period of time; 2 hours is usually ample. For pasta and rice dishes, cooked rice or pasta should be added during the last hour to half-hour of cooking time.

Fish and Seafood

When cooking a whole fish, it is a good idea to line the cooker with a piece of baking paper large enough to reach up the side, then place the fish on top. This makes lifting out the cooked fish much easier.

I have found cooking seafood highly successful in the slow cooker; it retains its shape, nutritional value and delicate flavour. It is ideal for squid, for instance, which benefits greatly from the slow-cooking process.

Vegetables

In the slow cooker, some vegetables tend to take longer to cook than meat. Generally speaking, root vegetables, such as carrots, parsnips and onions, should be cut into pieces no larger than 2 centimetres.

Soft vegetables, such as tomatoes and zucchini, should be added in the last hour of cooking, unless you want them to break down. Frozen vegetables should be thawed and added during the last half-hour.

Green vegetables, such as peas and beans, lose their characteristic bright colour if slow cooked.

Dried beans should be soaked overnight, and some beans, such as red kidney beans, need to be cooked for 15 minutes and drained before adding to the cooker. Certain varieties of dried beans can be poisonous if not cooked first. If you are unsure about the type of bean you are using, it is best to cook them in this way before using them in a slow cooker recipe.

I often use drained canned chickpeas or beans, and add them during the last hour to half-hour of cooking time.

Herbs and Spices

During cooking, herbs and spices may diminish in flavour. This particularly applies to dried herbs, so it is better to use fresh. I often use a combination of both. If you think the dish could do with a little more flavour when tasting at the end of the cooking time, just add extra at this point.

Be careful with adding cayenne pepper and Tabasco sauce — they can become bitter over a long period of cooking. Add them towards the end.

Dairy Products

Dairy products do not handle long periods of slow-cooking particularly well. Generally, they should be added during the last hour to half-hour of cooking.

Cheese or white sauces reputedly break down, though I have not found this to be a real issue if a combination of cornflour and eggs is added to the sauce mixture.

Low-fat cream or evaporated milk can be used instead of regular cream, and sometimes they perform better than the full-fat varieties.

Meat

Cheaper cuts of meat, such as casserole steaks, are a good choice for the slow cooker, as they break down to become very tender indeed.

Some people brown meat before adding it to the cooker. Generally, this is not necessary (I certainly don't bother), not even for roasts — it will just take extra time and effort and means extra cleaning up. For recipes in this book, I have eliminated the need to brown meat for the sake of convenience. The exception is Steak and Kidney Pudding, which is more about the thickening of the gravy than the browning of the meat.

However, if you want to sear the meat first, then that's fine too. If you have the luxury of a cooker insert that gives this option, by all means include this step if you want.

All visible fat and gristle should be cut off meat for the slow cooker. Use smaller whole roasts or cut a roast beef, for example, to fit comfortably in the cooker. Any lean trimmings from the meat can be used later in a casserole-type dish.

Meat should be thawed before placing in the cooker. This is because foods should reach 60°C (140°F) as soon as possible, and the inclusion of frozen meat could hamper this process.

Roasting meats is simple – just place them straight into the slow cooker. No liquid is necessary – the gravy develops during the cooking process. Herbs and spices can be used to season the meat if desired.

In some recipes an amount of sausage meat will be specified. Instead of buying sausage mince especially, use the required weight in sausages. Simply slit the skins lengthways and they easily peel off, leaving the filling ready to use.

To heat frankfurters or similar in the slow cooker, just pour in about ½ cup of water and place the frankfurters in the cooker. Heat on High or Low until hot enough to serve.

Chicken

For whole chicken, use a chicken no larger than 1.5 kilograms.

Although not absolutely necessary, for best results remove skin and visible fat from chicken. Opinions now vary on whether it is necessary to cook chicken on High — some manufacturers' instruction booklets indicate this should be so, others indicate that to cook chicken on Low is perfectly fine. Always check your cooker's instruction booklet to be sure. What I do is cook the chicken dish on High at the outset — even if only for a few minutes or half an hour, then reduce the setting to Low and cook for several hours more as indicated in the recipe.

Stocks

Slow-cooking is an ideal way to make stocks and saves buying expensive commercially made preparations. However, for convenience use those by all means or even a good-quality stock powder mixed with water (¾ teaspoon per cup of liquid).

Desserts

It is always a good idea to preheat the cooker for a few minutes on High before adding a pudding, especially if the recipe contains self-raising flour so that the raising ingredient is activated.

Desserts cooked in the slow cooker are always moist and delicious. Fruits tend to keep their shape well and the flavours are intensified. Self-saucing puddings cook to perfection.

SOUPS

CHICKEN AND VEGETABLE SOUP

Serves 4–6

(for a 3.2–4.5 litre slow cooker)

You can vary the vegetables used in this recipe. Personally, I like about ½ cup of fresh or thawed frozen peas added about 30 minutes from the end of cooking time.

600g chicken drumsticks
2 onions
1 leek, white part only (optional)
½ red capsicum, deseeded
1 large stalk celery
2 carrots
420g can creamed corn
2 cups chicken or vegetable stock (or 2 cups water with
    2 teaspoons stock powder)
garlic bread, to serve

Remove the skin from the chicken legs (it should just pull back – it doesn't matter if a little is left on), and place the legs in the slow cooker.

Dice the vegetables and add to the cooker with the creamed corn and stock.

Place the lid on the cooker and cook for 4 hours on High or 7–8 hours on Low.

Remove the drumsticks and shred the meat, returning this to the cooker. Add salt and pepper to taste.

This soup is nice served with garlic bread.

CREAM OF CAULIFLOWER AND LEEK SOUP

Serves 6
(for a 3.5–4.5 litre slow cooker)

The main part of this soup is cooked in the slow cooker. About 5 minutes work at the end involves making a quick cheese sauce that is stirred into the slow cooker to make a delicious creamy soup.

    250g leeks, white part only, diced
    1 cauliflower, roughly chopped
    4 cups chicken or vegetable stock (or 4 cups water with
        3 teaspoons stock powder)
    ¾ cup milk
    1 cup cream
    1 tablespoon cornflour mixed to a paste with ¼ cup milk
    1 cup grated tasty cheese
    1–2 teaspoons chicken or vegetable stock powder
        (optional)

Place the leek, cauliflower, and stock in the slow cooker, cover with the lid and cook for 4 hours on High or 7–8 hours on Low. Purée with a stick blender.

In a saucepan, combine the milk and cream and bring to the boil, stirring occasionally. Mix in the cornflour paste, stirring with a whisk until thickened. Stir in the cheese until melted. Add the stock powder, if using, or salt and pepper to taste. Stir into the cauliflower soup.

CREAM OF PARSNIP AND BACON SOUP

Serves 4–6
(for a 3.5–4.5 litre slow cooker)

The sweetness of parsnip is contrasted beautifully by the saltiness of bacon in this soup. If I have the time and inclination, I sauté 2 tablespoons of diced bacon in a little oil and sprinkle over the top of each bowl of soup to garnish.

> 1 leek (or small onion), white part only
> 750g parsnips
> 1 large onion, diced
> 125g lean bacon, rind removed, diced, plus extra to
>   serve (optional)
> 4 cups chicken stock (or 4 cups water with 2 teaspoons
>   stock powder)
> ¼ teaspoon salt (optional)
> ⅓ cup pouring or thickened cream
> chopped parsley, to serve (optional)

Wash the leek well, then dice. Peel the parsnips and chop into 2cm pieces. If there is any tough core, remove it and, if possible, replace its weight with more parsnip.

Place the leek and parsnip in the slow cooker with the onion, bacon, stock and salt. Cover with the lid and cook for 4 hours on High or 7–8 hours on Low. Mix in the cream and add salt and pepper to taste.

Serve topped with a little chopped parsley and/or crispy bacon pieces.

Goulash Soup

Serves 6–8

(for a 4.5–5 litre slow cooker)

This hearty soup is great for a winter's day, ideal to set and forget when you leave home for recreational activities or work. When you come home you can add the dumplings if liked, but this is by no means necessary. It is really a meal unto itself and is delicious served with fresh crusty bread or garlic bread.

600g beef cheeks or chuck or blade steak
2 x 400g cans diced tomatoes (or 800g fresh or bottled
   tomatoes)
3 cloves garlic, crushed
2 onions, diced
90g mushrooms, diced
1 large capsicum, deseeded and diced
1 carrot, diced
1 stalk celery, diced (optional)
2 tablespoons tomato paste
2 tablespoons tomato sauce (ketchup)
1 teaspoon brown sugar
1 tablespoon sweet chilli sauce
1 teaspoon Dijon mustard
2½ cups chicken, beef or vegetable stock (or 2½ cups
   water with 1½ teaspoons stock power)
2 sprigs fresh thyme or ½ teaspoon dried thyme
1 teaspoon salt (optional)

Herb Dumplings (optional)

2 teaspoons butter, softened
1 cup self-raising flour
¼ teaspoon salt
1 tablespoon snipped chives
1 tablespoon chopped parsley
milk or water to mix

Remove all visible fat from the meat and cut into small dice. Place in the slow cooker with the rest of the soup ingredients and stir to combine. Place the lid on the cooker and cook for 5 hours on High or 10 hours on Low. Add salt and pepper to taste.

To make the dumplings, rub the butter into the flour and salt with your fingertips (or do this in the food processor). Mix in the herbs and then add enough milk or water to make a soft dough. Shape teaspoonfuls of the dough into small balls.

Drop the dumplings into the simmering soup. Grease a piece of baking paper slightly larger than the cooker and place, greased side down, over the top of the cooker. Replace the lid and cook for 20 minutes more on High until the dumplings are puffed and light.

Herbed Pumpkin and Bacon Soup

Serves 6
(for a 3.5–4.5 litre slow cooker)

800g dark-fleshed pumpkin (such as kent, jap or butternut),
    peeled and diced
125g lean bacon, rind removed, diced
1 large onion, diced
2 cups chicken stock (or 2 cups water with 1½ teaspoons
    stock powder)
2 tablespoons chopped parsley, plus 1 tablespoon extra
2 teaspoons chopped thyme
1 cup milk
2 teaspoons tomato paste
1 teaspoon Dijon mustard
½ teaspoon salt (optional)
½ cup grated parmesan cheese

Place the pumpkin, bacon, onion, stock, parsley, thyme, milk, tomato paste, mustard and salt in the slow cooker.

Place the lid on the cooker and cook for 4 hours on High or 7–8 hours on Low.

Purée the soup using a stick blender. Mix in the extra parsley and the parmesan and stir until the cheese has melted. Add salt and pepper to taste.

ITALIAN MUSHROOM SOUP

Serves 4
(for a 3.2–3.5 litre slow cooker)

400g mushrooms, thinly sliced
2½ cups chicken stock (or 2½ cups water with
    1½ teaspoons stock power)
1 onion, diced
2 cloves garlic, crushed
1½ tablespoons dry or medium-dry sherry
1½ tablespoons tomato paste
¾ teaspoon salt (optional)
3 egg yolks
½ cup cream
⅓ cup finely grated parmesan cheese

Place the mushrooms, stock, onion, garlic, sherry, tomato paste and salt in the slow cooker and cover with the lid. Cook for 4 hours on High or 7–8 hours on Low.

Turn the cooker to High (if set on Low). Whisk together the egg yolks, cream and parmesan and stir into the soup to thicken slightly. Add salt and pepper to taste.

Cauliflower, Carrot and Cumin Soup

Serves 6
(for a 3.5–4.5 litre slow cooker)

½ cauliflower, 450g approximately
2 onions, diced
800g carrots, diced
2½ cups chicken or vegetable stock (or 2½ cups water with
     1½ teaspoons stock powder)
2 teaspoons ground cumin
3 teaspoons fish sauce
1 tablespoon tomato sauce (ketchup)
1 tablespoon sweet chilli sauce
3 teaspoons cornflour mixed to a paste with 1 tablespoon
     cold water
1 cup grated tasty cheese
½ cup grated parmesan cheese
½ cup cream
chopped parsley or coriander, to serve

Cut the cauliflower into small florets and place in the base of the slow cooker. Add the onion and carrot.

Mix together the stock, cumin and sauces and pour over the vegetables. Do not stir or the cauliflower on the surface may discolour to an unattractive brown as it is exposed to the air.

Place the lid on the cooker and cook for 4 hours on High or 7–8 hours on Low.

Purée the soup with a stick blender. Mix in the cornflour paste and cook for 5 minutes on High, then stir in the cheeses and cream. Replace the lid and cook for a further 3 minutes on High, or until the cheese has melted. Add salt and pepper to taste.

Serve sprinkled with the parsley or coriander.

LENTIL SOUP WITH CHORIZO

Serves 6
(for a 4–4.5 litre slow cooker)

250g chorizo, diced
125g lean bacon, rind removed, diced
300g dried red lentils
5 cups chicken stock (or 5 cups water and 2 teaspoons
    stock powder)
2 onions, diced
2 carrots, diced

Place all the ingredients in the slow cooker and stir to combine.

Place the lid on the cooker and cook for 4–5 hours on High or 8–10 hours on Low. Add salt and pepper to taste.

CREAM OF CARROT SOUP

Serves 4
(for a 3.2–3.5 litre slow cooker)

1kg carrots
2 onions
4 cups chicken stock (or 4 cups water with 2 teaspoons
    stock powder)
2 teaspoons sweet paprika
½ teaspoon brown sugar
½ teaspoon salt (optional)
½ cup cream

Chop the carrots and onions into 1.25cm pieces and place in the slow cooker. Add the stock, paprika, sugar and salt and stir to combine.

Place the lid on the cooker and cook for 4 hours on High or 7–8 hours on Low.

Purée the soup with a stick blender, then stir in the cream. Add salt and pepper to taste.

OXTAIL SOUP WITH BARLEY

Serves 8
(for a 3.5–4.5 litre slow cooker)

750g oxtail pieces
2 onions, diced
2 carrots, diced
1 stalk celery, diced
125g lean bacon, rind removed, diced
½ cup pearl barley
½ teaspoon salt (optional)
4 cups chicken or beef stock (or 4 cups water with
    3 teaspoons stock powder)

Place all the ingredients in the slow cooker. Stir to combine.

Place the lid on the cooker and cook for 5 hours on High or 10 hours on Low. Add salt and pepper to taste.

PUMPKIN, SWEET POTATO AND APPLE SOUP

Serves 6

(for a 3.2–4.5 litre slow cooker)

500g diced sweet potato
1 cooking apple (such as Granny Smith), peeled, cored and
   diced
500g diced pumpkin
1 large onion, diced
2 cups chicken or vegetable stock (or 2 cups water with
   1½ teaspoons stock powder)
1 teaspoon salt (optional)
½ cup cream (optional)
⅔ cup grated tasty cheese (optional)
white pepper, to taste

Place the sweet potato in the base of the slow cooker, then add the apple, followed by the rest of the ingredients.

Place the lid on the cooker and cook for 4–5 hours on High or 8–9 hours on Low.

Purée the soup with a stick blender. Stir in the cream and cheese, if using. Add salt and white pepper to taste.

Italian Tomato and Basil Soup with Meatballs

Serves 6
(for a 3.5–4.5 litre slow cooker)

2 x 400g cans diced tomatoes

1 onion

10 basil leaves

2 cloves garlic, crushed

1 teaspoon salt

2 teaspoons Worcestershire sauce

2 teaspoons sweet chilli sauce or 1 long red chilli,
    deseeded and roughly chopped

2 teaspoons tomato sauce (ketchup)

2 cups chicken stock (or 2 cups water with 1½ teaspoons
    stock powder)

½ teaspoon brown sugar

Meatballs

250g pork and veal mince

1 small onion, grated

1 slice of bread, crumbed

1 egg yolk

1 teaspoon soy sauce

1 teaspoon Worcestershire sauce

2 teaspoons smooth-textured chutney (any sort)

½ teaspoon salt

¼ cup grated parmesan cheese, plus extra, to serve

¼ teaspoon finely grated lemon rind (optional)

crusty bread or garlic bread, to serve

Place all the soup ingredients in the bowl of a food processor and process until smooth. Pour into the slow cooker. Turn the cooker onto High and heat while the meatballs are being made.

To make the meatballs, mix all the ingredients together until well combined. Roll teaspoonfuls of the mixture into balls and place in the liquid in the cooker.

Place the lid on the cooker and cook for 4 hours on High or 7–8 hours on Low.

Serve with a little extra parmesan sprinkled on top and some fresh crusty bread or garlic bread.

SCOTCH BROTH

Serves 6
(for a 3.5–4.5 litre slow cooker)

800g lamb forequarter pieces or chops
¼ cup pearl barley
2 onions, diced
2 carrots, diced
1 parsnip, diced
1 stalk celery, diced
5 cups chicken or vegetable stock (or 5 cups water with
    2 teaspoons stock powder)
¾ teaspoon salt
fresh crusty bread, to serve

Trim all visible fat from the meat and place in the slow cooker, along with
the rest of the ingredients. Cover with the lid and cook for 4 hours on
High or 8 hours on Low, or until the meat is falling off the bones.

Remove the meat pieces from the cooker with a slotted spoon. Shred
the meat, discarding the bones, and return the meat to the soup. Add
salt and pepper to taste.

Serve with fresh crusty bread.

MULLIGATAWNY SOUP

Serves 6
(for a 3.5–4.5 litre slow cooker)

500g chicken pieces, fat and skin removed
½ cup dried red lentils
2 onions, diced
2 carrots, diced
2 stalks celery, diced
2 teaspoons curry powder
1 teaspoon sweet paprika
½ teaspoon garam masala
1 teaspoon grated green ginger root
2 cloves garlic, crushed
1 long red chilli or 3 teaspoons sweet chilli sauce (optional)
2 teaspoons Worcestershire sauce
2 teaspoons chutney (any sort)
4 cups chicken stock (or 4 cups water with 3 teaspoons
    stock powder)
65ml coconut milk
crusty bread or naan, to serve

Place all the ingredients in the slow cooker. Cover with the lid and cook for 4 hours on High or 8 hours on Low.

Remove the chicken from the cooker and dice or shred the meat, discarding the bones. Return the chicken to the slow cooker. Add salt and pepper to taste.

Serve with fresh crusty bread or naan.

SWEET POTATO AND CORIANDER SOUP

Serves 4–6

(for a 3.5–4.5 litre slow cooker)

800g sweet potato

1 onion, diced

1 clove garlic, crushed

1 tablespoon fish sauce

3 cups chicken stock (or 3 cups water with 2 teaspoons
    stock powder)

¼ teaspoon ground cumin

4 tablespoons chopped coriander

65ml coconut milk

Peel the sweet potato, cut into 2cm cubes and add to the slow cooker
with the onion, garlic, fish sauce, stock, cumin and 2 tablespoons of the
coriander. Stir to combine.

Place the lid on the cooker and cook for 4 hours on High or 8–9 hours on
Low.

Purée the soup with a stick blender.

Stir in the remaining coriander and the coconut milk and cook for
10 minutes more on High. Add salt and pepper to taste.

SWISS CHICKEN SOUP

Serves 4

(for a 3.2–3.5 litre slow cooker)

250–300g skinless chicken breast fillets

90g sliced ham

2 onions

1 tablespoon Dijon mustard

4 cups chicken stock (or 4 cups water with 2½ teaspoons
 stock powder)

410g can creamed corn

2 teaspoons cornflour mixed to a paste with 3 teaspoons
 cold water

1 cup grated tasty cheese

½ cup cream

4 egg yolks

crusty bread, to serve

Finely dice the chicken, ham and onions. Place in the slow cooker with
the mustard, stock and corn. Stir to combine, place the lid on the cooker
and cook for 4 hours on High or 8 hours on Low.

Stir the cornflour paste into the soup and cook for 5 minutes on High,
then stir in the cheese until melted.

Whisk together the cream and egg yolks and mix into the soup. Add
salt and pepper to taste. Replace the lid and cook for 5 minutes more
on High.

Serve with fresh crusty bread.

CREAM OF CELERIAC AND PARSNIP SOUP

Serves 4–6

(for a 4.5–5 litre slow cooker)

2kg celeriac, approximately
3 teaspoons olive oil
1 tablespoon lemon juice
300g parsnips
1 onion
1 leek, white part only
3 cloves garlic
4 cups chicken or vegetable stock (or 4 cups water with
    3 teaspoons stock powder)
1 cup cream
white pepper, to taste

Cut the top and base from the celeriac and peel. Cut into 1.25cm cubes and place in the slow cooker. Add the olive oil and lemon juice and stir to coat the celeriac (this stops it discolouring).

Peel the parsnips and cut into 1cm chunks, dice the onion and leek, chop the garlic and add them all to the cooker, together with the stock. Do not stir.

Place the lid on the cooker and cook for 6–7 hours on High or 10–11 hours on Low.

Purée the soup with a stick blender, then stir in the cream and add salt and white pepper to taste.

ROASTED RED CAPSICUM AND PUMPKIN SOUP

Serves 6
(for a 3.5–4.5 litre slow cooker)

1kg dark-fleshed pumpkin (such as jap or butternut)
500g red capsicums
1 tablespoon tomato paste
3 cups chicken stock (or 3 cups water with 2 teaspoons
    stock powder)
1 teaspoon paprika
½ cup coconut cream
½ cup cream

Peel the pumpkin and cut the flesh into 3cm dice.

Cut the capsicums into quarters and remove the seeds then roast, skin side up, under a hot grill until the skin blackens. Wrap in plastic wrap until cool enough to handle, then remove and discard the skin.

Add the capsicum to the slow cooker with the pumpkin, tomato paste, stock and paprika. Place the lid on the cooker and cook for 4–5 hours on High or 8–9 hours on Low.

Purée the soup with a stick blender. Stir in the coconut cream and cream and add salt and pepper to taste.

THAI CHICKEN, CORN AND CHILLI SOUP

Serves 4

(for a 3.2–4 litre slow cooker)

400ml tin coconut milk

1 cup chicken stock (or 1 cup water with ½ teaspoon
    stock powder)

1 tablespoon lime juice

rind of ½ lime, grated

125g button mushrooms, sliced thinly

1½ teaspoons grated fresh green ginger

3 teaspoons fish sauce

2 teaspoons sweet chilli sauce

1 cup creamed corn

½ cup corn kernels

3 long red chillies, seeds removed and finely chopped

250g skinless chicken breast fillet, diced

Place all the ingredients in the slow cooker and stir to combine. Place
the lid on the cooker and cook for 3 hours on High or 5–6 hours on Low.
Add salt and white pepper to taste.

VEGETABLES AND MOSTLY VEGETARIAN

CIDER BRAISED ONIONS

Serves 4–6 as a side dish
(for a 3.2–3.5 litre slow cooker)

If pickling onions are hard to access, simply use the smallest ones you can find.

> 750g pickling onions, peeled
> ½ cup dry or medium-dry cider
> ¾ teaspoon Dijon mustard
> 1 teaspoon sugar
> ½ teaspoon salt

Place the onions in the slow cooker. Mix the rest of the ingredients together and pour over the onions.

Place the lid on the cooker and cook for 3 hours on High or 6 hours on Low.

COURTNEY'S LENTIL AND VEGETABLE RAGOUT

Serves 6 as a main course, 10 as a side dish
(for a 4.5–5 litre slow cooker)

A hearty and healthy meal for vegetarians or a side dish to feed many.

125g dried red lentils
2 onions, diced
350g sweet potato, diced
400g eggplant, cut into 1cm cubes
200g zucchini, cut into 1cm cubes
2 carrots, diced
400g can diced tomatoes
3 teaspoons tomato paste
3 cups vegetable stock (or 3 cups water with 2 teaspoons
   stock powder)
3 teaspoons sweet chilli sauce
1½ tablespoons tomato sauce (ketchup)
400g can chickpeas, drained and rinsed
400g can three bean mix or kidney beans, drained and
   rinsed
1 teaspoon quince jelly or brown sugar
couscous or steamed or boiled rice, to serve

Place all the ingredients in the slow cooker and stir to combine. Place the lid on the cooker and cook for 4 hours on High or 7–8 hours on Low. Add salt and pepper to taste.

Serve on couscous or rice.

MIDDLE EASTERN RICE

Serves 4–6
(for a 3.2–3.5 litre slow cooker)

2 cups long-grain rice
½ cup pine nuts
½ cup currants
4 cups chicken stock (or 4 cups water with 3 teaspoons
    stock powder)
½ teaspoon ground turmeric
2 tablespoons chopped parsley
4 silverbeet or 2 cups baby English spinach leaves,
    shredded

Place the rice, pine nuts, currants, stock and turmeric in the slow cooker and stir to combine. Place the lid on the cooker and cook for 1½–2 hours on High or 3 hours on Low.

Stir in the parsley and silverbeet or spinach. Replace the lid on the cooker and cook for 10 minutes more. Add salt and pepper to taste.

CAPONATA

Serves 4–6
(for a 3.2–4.5 litre slow cooker)

This delicious, tasty dish is ideal for vegetarians or as a side dish. Serve with fresh crusty bread or garlic bread.

    500g eggplant
    2 onions
    1 stalk celery
    20 black olives
    400g can diced tomatoes
    5 teaspoons capers in brine, drained
    2 tablespoons pine nuts (optional)
    1 tablespoon tomato paste
    ¼ cup sugar
    ⅓ cup white vinegar
    1 tablespoon sweet chilli sauce
    1 teaspoon salt (optional)

Cut the eggplant into 1.5cm cubes and place in the slow cooker.

Dice the onions and slice the celery into 1cm lengths. Add to the slow cooker with the rest of the ingredients and stir to mix.

Place the lid on the cooker and cook for 4 hours on High or 7–8 hours on Low. Add salt and pepper to taste.

LEEKY THYME POTATOES

Serves 4–6
(for a 3.5–4.5 litre slow cooker)

1.5kg potatoes (such as kennebecs or bintjes)
2 large leeks, white part only
½ teaspoon salt
2 tablespoons chopped thyme
1 cup chicken or vegetable stock (or 1 cup water with
    ¾ teaspoon stock powder)
30g butter, melted
1½ teaspoons cornflour mixed to a paste with 1 tablespoon
    cold water (optional)
2 tablespoons cream (optional)

Peel and thinly slice the potatoes.

Wash and slice the leeks.

Place a layer of a third of the potato slices in the slow cooker, sprinkle with some of the salt, top with a layer of half the leeks and half the thyme. Repeat layering, then finish with the remaining potato slices. Pour in the stock and press down slightly so that as much potato as possible is covered with the liquid.

Brush the top layer of potato with the melted butter.

Place the lid on the cooker and cook for 4 hours on High or 8 hours on Low.

Remove the lid and stir in some or all of the cornflour paste to thicken, if needed. Stir in the cream, if using. Add salt and pepper to taste.

MUSHROOM AND BACON RISOTTO

Serves 4
(for a 3.5–4.5 litre slow cooker)

By conventional cooking methods arborio rice would be used. However, this goes too gluggy in the slow cooker so long-grain rice is used here. You may need to use a little extra stock at the end.

    1 onion, finely diced
    250g mushrooms, sliced
    2 cloves garlic, crushed
    200g lean bacon, rind removed, diced
    1 cup long-grain rice
    juice of ½ large lemon
    2½ cups chicken or vegetable stock (or 2½ cups water with
        1 teaspoon stock powder)
    3 teaspoons chopped thyme
    ½ cup chopped semi-dried tomatoes
    ½ teaspoon salt (optional)
    ½ cup pouring or thickened cream
    ½ cup grated or shaved parmesan cheese
    45g butter, diced
    1–2 tablespoons chopped parsley, to serve

Place the onion, mushrooms, garlic, bacon, rice, lemon juice, stock, thyme, tomatoes and salt in the slow cooker and stir to combine.

Place the lid on the cooker and cook for 2 hours on High or 4 hours on Low.

Stir in the cream, parmesan and butter. Add salt and pepper to taste.

Sprinkle with the chopped parsley to serve.

49

POTATOES BOULANGERE WITH BACON

Serves 4
(for a 3.5–4.5 litre slow cooker)

600g potatoes
2 onions
125g bacon, rind removed
2 tablespoons chopped parsley
½ teaspoon salt, approximately (optional)
1 cup chicken stock (or 1 cup water with ½ teaspoon stock
 powder)

Peel the potatoes and onions and cut into thin slices (about 6mm). Dice the bacon.

Layer in the slow cooker as follows:
 one-third of the potato slices;
 half the onion;
 a light sprinkling of salt, if using;
 one-third of the bacon;
 one-third of the parsley;
 one-third of the potato slices;
 the remaining onion;
 a light sprinkling of salt, if using;
 one-third of the bacon;
 one-third of the parsley;
 the remaining potato slices;
 a light sprinkling of salt, if using;
 the remaining bacon;
 the remaining parsley.

Pour the stock over the top. Cover the cooker with the lid and cook for 3 hours on High or 5–6 hours on Low approximately until the potato is cooked through. Add salt and pepper to taste.

POTATO AND CAULIFLOWER CURRY

Serves 4–6

(for a 3.2–3.5 litre slow cooker)

600g potatoes
450g cauliflower
3 cloves garlic, crushed
2 onions, diced
2 tomatoes, diced
3 teaspoons mustard powder
3 teaspoons ground cumin
½ teaspoon garam masala
½ teaspoon brown sugar
1 teaspoon vegetable stock powder
½ teaspoon salt
1 tablespoon sweet chilli sauce
¼ cup dry or medium-dry apple cider
¾ cup water
1 tablespoon tomato sauce (ketchup)
65ml coconut milk
2 teaspoons cornflour mixed to a paste with 1 tablespoon
    cold water (optional)
¼ cup chopped coriander (optional)
boiled or steamed rice or couscous, to serve

Peel the potatoes and cut into 2cm cubes. Place in the base of the slow cooker.

Cut the cauliflower into florets (not too small) and place over the potatoes, together with the garlic, onion and tomato.

Mix together the mustard, cumin, garam masala, sugar, stock powder, salt, sweet chilli sauce, cider, water, tomato sauce and coconut milk and pour over the vegetables.

Place the lid on the cooker and cook for 3–4 hours on High or 7 hours on Low.

If needed, thicken with some or all of the cornflour paste. Mix in the coriander, if using, and add salt and pepper to taste.

Serve over plain rice or couscous.

PEPPERED RICE WITH PEAS

Serves 4–6
(for a 3.2–4.5 litre slow cooker)

1 red capsicum
1 green capsicum
1½ cups long-grain rice
1 onion, diced
½ teaspoon salt
3 cups vegetable or chicken stock (or 3 cups water with
    2 teaspoons stock powder)
1 cup fresh or frozen peas
2 tablespoons chopped parsley
30g butter, diced

Remove the seeds and cores from the capsicums and dice. Place in the slow cooker with the rice, onion, salt and stock. Stir to combine.

Place the lid on the cooker and cook for 2 hours on High or 3–3½ hours on Low.

Near the end of the cooking time, pour boiling water over the peas in a heatproof bowl, then strain off the liquid. Add the peas to the slow cooker with the parsley and stir to combine. Cook for 20 minutes more. Stir in the butter. Add salt and pepper to taste.

HERBED PUMPKIN CASSEROLE

Serves 4
(for a 3.2–3.5 litre slow cooker)

750g pumpkin (such as kent, jap or butternut)
1 apple, peeled, cored and diced (such as golden delicious
    or Granny Smith)
125g lean bacon, rind removed, diced
1 onion, diced
juice of ½ orange
1½ cups chicken or vegetable stock (or 1½ cups water with
    1 teaspoon stock powder)
1 tablespoon chopped parsley, plus 1 tablespoon extra
1 teaspoon chopped thyme
3 teaspoons cornflour mixed to a paste with
    1½ tablespoons cold water

Peel the pumpkin, remove and discard any seeds and cut into 2.5cm cubes. Place in the slow cooker with the apple, bacon, onion, orange juice, stock, parsley and thyme. Stir to mix well. Place the lid on the cooker and cook for 3 hours on High or 6 hours on Low.

If the casserole needs thickening, mix in some or all of the cornflour paste. Stir in the extra parsley and add salt and pepper to taste.

Ratatouille

Serves 6
(for a 3.2–3.5 litre slow cooker)

2 onions
1 small eggplant
300g zucchini
1 red (or green) capsicum, deseeded
120g mushrooms
3 cloves garlic, crushed
400g can diced tomatoes
2 teaspoons sweet paprika
3 teaspoons sweet chilli sauce
2 teaspoons Worcestershire sauce
3 teaspoons chutney (any sort)
1 tablespoon tomato paste
1½ teaspoons brown sugar
1½ teaspoons salt
2–3 sprigs rosemary
pasta, couscous or polenta, to serve
crusty bread, to serve

Dice the onion and cut the eggplant, zucchini and capsicum into 1cm cubes. Slice the mushrooms. Place the vegetables in the slow cooker with the rest of the ingredients and stir to combine. Cover with the lid and cook for 3 hours on High or 6 hours on Low. Add salt and pepper to taste.

Serve as a vegetarian dish with pasta, couscous or polenta and fresh crusty bread.

Note: *This is also good used as a pizza topping, topped with slices of mozzarella and torn basil leaves.*

RED CABBAGE WITH ORANGE AND CARAWAY SEEDS

Serves 4–6 as a side dish
(for a 3.2–3.5 litre slow cooker)

½ red cabbage (about 1.25kg), finely shredded

1 onion, diced

2 teaspoons grated orange rind

juice of 1 orange

1 tablespoon balsamic vinegar

3 teaspoons brown sugar

1 teaspoon golden syrup

1 teaspoon caraway seeds

1 teaspoon salt or chicken stock powder

3 teaspoons cornflour mixed to a paste with
    1½ tablespoons cold water (optional)

Place all the ingredients except the cornflour paste in the slow cooker and stir to combine. Cover with the lid and cook for 3 hours on High or 6 hours on Low.

Thicken, if needed, with some or all of the cornflour paste and add salt and pepper to taste.

ROOT VEGETABLE PURÉE

Serves 4–6 as a side dish
(for a 3.2–3.5 litre slow cooker)

The combination of root vegetables in this dish is really delicious. However, you can vary it to include any other root vegetables.

180g carrots
500g parsnips
80g swede or turnip
300g sweet potato
¾ cup chicken or vegetable stock (or ¾ cup water with
    ½ teaspoon stock powder)
½ teaspoon salt
50g butter, diced

Peel the vegetables and cut into 3cm cubes. Place in the slow cooker with the stock and salt. Cover with the lid and cook for 4 hours on High or 7–8 hours on Low.

Mash the mixture until very smooth or purée with a stick blender. Whisk in the butter. Add salt and pepper to taste.

Note: *For a really rich and even more delicious dish, add ½ cup grated tasty cheese and 2 tablespoons cream at the end of cooking time.*

VEGETABLE CASSEROLE

Serves 6

(for a 3.5–4.5 litre slow cooker)

750g sweet potato

120g carrots

2 onions

100g parsnip

150g tomatoes, diced

1 red capsicum, deseeded and diced

2 tablespoons tomato paste

juice of ½ small lemon

¾ teaspoon salt

3 teaspoons tomato sauce (ketchup)

3 teaspoons sweet chilli sauce

1 cup vegetable stock (or 1 cup water with 1 teaspoon
   stock powder)

3 teaspoons cornflour mixed to a paste with 1 tablespoon
   cold water

Peel the sweet potato, carrots, onions and parsnip and cut into 1cm cubes. Place in the slow cooker with the tomato, capsicum, tomato paste, lemon juice, salt, sauces and stock. Stir to combine. Cover with the lid and cook for 4 hours on High or 7–8 hours on Low. Turn the cooker to High (if set on Low) and stir in all the cornflour paste to thicken, if needed. Add salt and pepper to taste.

VEGETABLE KORMA

Serves 4

(for a 3.2–4.5 litre slow cooker)

300g potatoes
200g sweet potato
100g pumpkin (such as kent, jap or butternut)
200g parsnips
2 onions
3 cloves garlic, crushed
3 teaspoons grated green ginger root
400ml can coconut milk
1½ tablespoons sweet chilli sauce
3 teaspoons ground cumin
1 teaspoon garam masala
1 teaspoon mustard powder
1½ teaspoons ground coriander
1 teaspoon salt
1½ tablespoons tomato paste
couscous and naan, to serve
Greek-style yoghurt, to serve

Peel the vegetables and cut into 1.5cm pieces. Place in the slow cooker with the rest of the ingredients and mix well.

Place the lid on the cooker and cook for 4–5 hours on High or 8–9 hours on Low. Add salt and pepper to taste.

Serve as a side dish or main vegetarian meal with couscous and naan and a little Greek-style yoghurt to the side.

VEGETABLES IN SPICY PEANUT SAUCE

Serves 4–6

(for a 3.5–4.5 litre slow cooker)

Excellent as a vegetarian meal or as a side dish.

> 500g washed potatoes
> 2 onions
> 400g sweet potato
> 1 parsnip, 250g approximately
> 2 teaspoons curry powder
> 1½ teaspoons ground cumin
> 1 teaspoon ground coriander
> 1 teaspoon salt
> juice of ½ lemon
> 1 tablespoon soy sauce
> 3 teaspoons sweet chilli sauce
> 4 rounded tablespoons peanut butter (crunchy or smooth)
> 400ml can coconut milk
> steamed or boiled rice or couscous and pappadums, to
>   serve

Cut the potatoes into 1cm cubes and place in the slow cooker. Peel and cut the onions, sweet potato and parsnip into 1cm cubes and add to the cooker, together with the spices, salt, lemon juice, sauces, peanut butter and coconut milk. Stir to combine.

Place the lid on the cooker and cook for 3 hours on High or 5–6 hours on Low. Add salt and pepper to taste.

Serve with plain rice or couscous and pappadums.

HUNGARIAN POTATOES

Serves 4–6 as a side dish
(for a 3.5–4.5 litre slow cooker)

This is a good, hearty side dish or even a main course vegetarian meal.

750g potatoes
1 onion
1 stalk celery
1 red capsicum
1 leek, white part only (optional)
2 cloves garlic, crushed
2 teaspoons paprika
3 teaspoons Worcestershire sauce
2 teaspoons olive oil
1¼ cups diced tomatoes (fresh, canned or bottled)
3 teaspoons tomato paste
3 teaspoons chutney (any sort)
1 teaspoon brown sugar
3 teaspoons chopped sage or thyme
1 teaspoon salt
2 rounded tablespoons sour cream
chopped parsley, to serve (optional)

Peel the potatoes and cut into 1.25cm cubes. Dice the onion and slice the celery. Deseed and dice the capsicum and slice the leek, if using. Place all the vegetables in the slow cooker with the rest of the ingredients except the sour cream and stir to combine.

Cover with the lid and cook for 4 hours on High or 7–8 hours on Low.

Stir in the sour cream, then add salt and pepper to taste.

Serve sprinkled with chopped parsley, if liked.

SPICED PUMPKIN PURÉE

Serves 6
(for a 3.2–3.5 litre slow cooker)

This delicious dish I find is best cooked on Low. It is an excellent side dish for meats or chicken.

1kg pumpkin
2 cloves garlic, crushed
½ cup dried red lentils
1 teaspoon ground coriander
2 teaspoons ground cumin
½ teaspoon mustard powder
½ teaspoon garam masala
1 tablespoon sweet chilli sauce
¾ cup coconut milk
¾ cup water
¾ teaspoon salt

Peel the pumpkin, remove and discard the seeds, then cut the flesh into 2.5cm cubes. Place in the slow cooker with the rest of the ingredients and stir to combine.

Place the lid on the cooker and cook for 4 hours on High or 7 hours on Low. Add salt and pepper to taste.

VEGETABLES FOR A ROAST

Serves 4
(for a 3.5–5 litre slow cooker)

This method of cooking vegetables makes a roast possible, even for the busiest of days. The vegetables are gently cooked all day long, then, a few minutes before serving, are quickly browned in a little oil on the stovetop. It reduces messy washing-up significantly and the vegetables are wonderfully flavoured. You can use different vegetables if you prefer, for example turnips, sweet potato, golden beets.

2 carrots
2 parsnips
4 small onions
4 cloves garlic
1kg pumpkin (such as kent, jap or butternut)
3 tablespoons water

Peel the vegetables, cut the carrots into chunks, not too thick (no more than 2.5cm), and place in the base of the slow cooker. Cut the parsnips into similar-sized pieces and place on top, then scatter the onions and garlic cloves around the cooker. Cut the pumpkin into large chunks or wedges and place on top. Pour in the water. Place the lid on the cooker and cook for 4 hours on High or 7–8 hours on Low.

A few minutes before serving, pour some oil to a depth of 8mm in a frying pan. Heat to 180°C approximately. Remove the vegetables from the cooker and cook in the oil on one side until browned, then turn over and brown on the other side. They are now ready to serve with your roast meat.

Note: *Use the liquid that remains in the base of the slow cooker to make a gravy if you need it, or add to a soup another time. (If using later, store in the fridge or freezer in an airtight container.)*

STUFFED TOMATOES

Serves 4
(for a 3.5–4.5 litre slow cooker)

500g firm tomatoes (about 4 tomatoes)
2 tablespoons water

Filling
1 small onion, grated
1½ tablespoons chopped parsley
100g bacon, rind removed, diced
2 teaspoons Worcestershire sauce
1 egg, lightly beaten
½ cup breadcrumbs
90g parmesan cheese, grated

Cut the tomatoes in half and scoop out the pulp and seeds.

Mix together the filling ingredients and fill the cavities in the tomatoes.

Pour the water into the base of the slow cooker and arrange the stuffed tomatoes on top.

Place the lid on the cooker and cook for 2 hours on High or 3½–4 hours on Low.

PUMPKIN TIMBALES WITH PARSLEY BUTTER

Serves 6
(for a 3.5–4.5 litre slow cooker)

½ cup milk
60g grated tasty cheese
30g grated parmesan cheese
2 eggs
¼ cup self-raising flour
½ cup cooked mashed pumpkin, cooled
½ cup creamed corn
¼ teaspoon salt
2 tomatoes
60g butter
1½ tablespoons finely chopped parsley

Heat the milk in a saucepan until boiling, then stir in the cheeses until melted.

In a bowl, whisk together the eggs, flour, pumpkin, corn and salt, then fold in the cheese mixture until well combined.

Grease six 200ml metal dariole moulds.

Cut the tomatoes into 8mm thick slices. Place a piece of tomato in the base of each mould (cutting to size if necessary).

Spoon the pumpkin mixture into each mould to two-thirds full. Place a slice of tomato on top. Place the moulds in the slow cooker and pour in boiling water to come halfway up the sides of the moulds.

Place the lid on the cooker and cook for 2½ hours on High or 5 hours on Low.

Remove the timbales with oven mitts and leave to stand in the moulds for 5 minutes, then turn out onto serving plates.

Melt the butter and add the parsley, then drizzle a little over each timbale before serving.

SPANISH POTATOES WITH CHORIZO AND BLACK OLIVES

Serves 4–6
(for a 3.5–4.5 litre slow cooker)

You can leave the chorizo out if preferred.

This dish makes a delicious sauce for pasta. Top each serve with shaved parmesan.

700g potatoes
1 large red capsicum
1 onion, diced
2 cloves garlic, crushed
½ teaspoon salt
1 teaspoon sugar
½ cup shredded basil leaves
2 teaspoons sweet paprika
3 teaspoons tomato paste
1 tablespoon tomato sauce (ketchup)
2 chorizos (about 250g), sliced
½ cup black olives

Peel the potatoes and cut into 1cm cubes. Remove the seeds and core from the capsicum and cut into 1cm pieces.

Place the potato and capsicum in the slow cooker with the rest of the ingredients and stir to combine. Cover with the lid and cook for 4 hours on High or 7–8 hours on Low. Add salt and pepper to taste.

TURKISH RISOTTO

Serves 4–6
(for a 3.5–4.5 litre slow cooker)

This dish is quite moist – a delicious accompaniment to a curry or casserole-style dish.

> 1½ cups long-grain rice
> 4 cups vegetable or chicken stock (or 4 cups water with
>   2½ teaspoons of stock powder)
> ½ cup chopped dried apricots
> ¼ cup currants
> ⅓ cup slivered almonds
> ½ teaspoon salt
> 1 teaspoon ground turmeric
> 1 onion, finely diced
> 1 stalk celery, finely diced
> 3 tablespoons chopped parsley

Place all the ingredients except the parsley in the slow cooker and stir to combine.

Place the lid on the cooker and cook for 2½–3 hours on High until the rice is tender.

Fluff up the rice with a fork while at the same time mixing through the chopped parsley. Add salt and pepper to taste.

BOMBAY POTATOES

Serves 4
(for a 3.2–3.5 litre slow cooker)

It is best to use a waxier-type potato for this recipe, or at least one that does not go to mush during cooking. Ask your vegetable supplier if in doubt.

Although the recipe specifies peeling the potatoes, you can use washed potatoes, in which case they need not be peeled.

1kg potatoes
1 onion, diced
2 teaspoons garam masala
2 teaspoons ground cumin
2 teaspoons ground coriander
1 teaspoon sweet paprika
1 teaspoon salt
3 teaspoons chutney (any sort)
3 teaspoons sweet chilli sauce
1 tablespoon tomato sauce (ketchup)
400g can diced tomatoes

Peel the potatoes and cut into 2cm dice. Place in the slow cooker with the rest of the ingredients and stir to combine, making sure that the potatoes are coated with the sauce.

Cover with the lid and cook for 3½–4 hours on High or 7–8 hours on Low. Add salt and pepper to taste.

RANCHER'S EGGS

Serves 4
(for a 3.2–3.5 litre slow cooker)

This delicious Mexican-style breakfast dish is very easy to prepare – and when put on the night before, requires only a few minutes in the morning to cook the eggs. It is generally served over corn tortillas but I often serve it over thick slices of lightly toasted sourdough bread.

600g canned diced tomatoes
1 onion, finely diced
½ red capsicum, deseeded and diced
2 cloves garlic, crushed
1 teaspoon ground cumin
¾ teaspoon ground oregano
3 teaspoons sweet chilli sauce
1 teaspoon vegetable or chicken stock powder
½ teaspoon brown sugar
¾ teaspoon salt
2 teaspoons cornflour mixed to a paste with 1 tablespoon
    cold water (optional)
4–6 eggs
corn tortillas, to serve
grated tasty cheese, to serve
refried beans, to serve (optional)

Place all the ingredients except the cornflour paste and eggs in the slow cooker, stir well to combine.

Cover with the lid and cook for 4 hours on High or 8–9 hours on Low. Add salt and pepper to taste.

If needed, thicken with some or all of the cornflour paste – you need to be able to make hollows in the mixture in which to sit the eggs. Break in the eggs, turn the cooker to High, cover with the lid and cook for a few minutes until the eggs are cooked to your liking.

Serve over tortillas sprinkled with cheese. Some people like to serve the eggs with refried beans, which are available at supermarkets.

Note: *To feed a crowd, use a larger cooker and double the recipe. The number of eggs that will fit in your cooker will determine the number of people you can feed.*

ROASTED RED CAPSICUM AND EGGPLANT LASAGNE

Serves 6
(for a 4.5–5 litre slow cooker)

700g red capsicums
500g eggplant
200g zucchini
1 onion
2 teaspoons salt
200g pumpkin
300g sweet potato
1 tablespoon chopped rosemary
2 x 400g cans diced tomatoes
3 teaspoons cornflour
2 cloves garlic, crushed
½ teaspoon brown sugar
1 teaspoon salt, extra
3 teaspoons chutney (any sort)
3 teaspoons sweet chilli sauce
400g fresh lasagne sheets
½ cup grated parmesan cheese
crusty bread or garlic bread and green salad, to serve

Cut the capsicums in half and remove the seeds and cores. Place under a hot grill, skin side up, until the skin blackens. Wrap in plastic wrap and leave to cool for a few minutes, by which time the skin will peel off easily.

Meanwhile, cut the eggplant, zucchini and onion into 8mm slices and place in a colander with the salt and mix well. Leave to stand for 30 minutes, then rinse and pat dry with paper towel.

Peel the pumpkin and sweet potato and cut into 6mm slices. Mix together.

Mix together the rosemary, tomatoes, cornflour, garlic, sugar, extra salt, chutney and sweet chilli sauce.

Place a layer of the sauce mixture in the base of the slow cooker, then add a layer of lasagne sheets and continue to layer as follows:

> eggplant, zucchini and onion mixture;
> pumpkin and sweet potato mixture;
> sauce mixture;
> lasagne sheets;
> eggplant, zucchini and onion mixture;
> pumpkin and sweet potato mixture;
> sauce mixture;
> lasagne sheets;
> sauce mixture.

Place the lid on the cooker and cook for 3½–4 hours on High or 7–8 hours on Low. Remove the lid from the cooker and sprinkle the parmesan on top. Cover with the lid and cook on High until the cheese has melted (about 5–10 minutes).

Serve with fresh crusty bread or garlic bread and green salad.

Napolitana Sauce

Serves 6
(for a 3.2–4.5 litre slow cooker)

This dish is ideal for serving with pasta. Any leftovers can be added to a gravy or soup or as a sauce to top a pizza.

1 large onion, diced
1 large red capsicum, deseeded and diced
4 cloves garlic, crushed
1 teaspoon apricot jam or brown sugar
1 tablespoon chopped fresh rosemary or basil
1 teaspoon vegetable stock powder
2 x 400g cans diced tomatoes
3 teaspoons soy sauce
3 teaspoons Worcestershire sauce
1 tablespoon tomato sauce (ketchup)
3 teaspoons chutney (any sort)
1 tablespoon sweet chilli sauce
3 teaspoons cornflour mixed to a paste with 2 tablespoons
     cold water (optional)
cooked pasta, to serve (any sort)
grated parmesan cheese, to serve

Place all the ingredients except the cornflour paste in the slow cooker, cover with the lid and cook for 4 hours on High or 8 hours on Low.

Thicken slightly, if needed, by stirring in the cornflour paste. Add salt and pepper to taste.

Serve over pasta and top with the grated parmesan.

FISH AND
OTHER SEAFOOD

FLATHEAD WITH SPICED POTATO CREAM

Serves 4–6
(for a 3.5–4.5 litre slow cooker)

The spice mixture seeps into the potatoes and leek, resulting in a delicious spiced cream that in no way overpowers the delicate flavour of the fish.

    350g potatoes, coarsely grated
    70g butter, melted
    1 leek, white part only, very thinly sliced
    600g flathead fillets, with skin
    1½ teaspoons mustard powder
    1½ teaspoons sweet paprika
    ½ teaspoon vegetable stock powder
    2 teaspoons brown sugar
    2 tablespoons lime juice
    2 tablespoons cream
    white pepper, to taste

Quickly mix together the grated potatoes and melted butter to stop the potatoes browning. Mix in the leek.

Grease the base of the slow cooker and cover with the potato mixture. Place the flathead fillets on top, skin side down.

Mix together the mustard powder, paprika, stock powder, sugar and lime juice and spoon over the fish. Place the lid on the cooker and cook on Low for 2½–3 hours, or until the fish is cooked. Remove the fish from the cooker and keep warm.

Mix the cream into the potato mixture, cover the cooker with the lid and cook for 5 minutes on High. Add salt and white pepper to taste. Serve portions of the fish on the spiced potato cream.

SEAFOOD LAKSA

Serves 4–6
(for a 4–4.5 litre slow cooker)

400g white fish fillets (such as ling or whiting)
200g calamari, cleaned
1 onion, finely diced
3cm piece of green ginger root, peeled and finely grated
4 cloves garlic, crushed
2 teaspoons finely chopped lemongrass, white part only, or
    ½ teaspoon finely grated lemon rind
2 teaspoons ground cumin
1½ teaspoons ground coriander
1 teaspoon ground turmeric
3 teaspoons fish sauce
3 teaspoons brown sugar
1 teaspoon smooth peanut butter (optional)
2 tablespoons lemon or lime juice
1½ teaspoons chicken or vegetable stock powder
400ml can coconut milk
200g uncooked medium-sized prawns, peeled and
    deveined with tail intact
400g fresh egg noodles
3 tablespoons chopped coriander leaves
1 long red chilli, deseeded and finely chopped, to serve
    (optional)

Cut the fish into 3cm pieces and slice the calamari thinly. Place in the slow cooker with the onion, ginger, garlic, lemongrass, spices, fish sauce, sugar, peanut butter, if using, lemon juice, stock powder and coconut milk and stir to combine. Cover with the lid and cook for 3 hours on Low.

Stir in the prawns and egg noodles and cook for 5–10 minutes.

Stir in half the coriander. Add salt and pepper to taste.

Serve bowls of laksa sprinkled with the remaining coriander and the chilli, if liked.

GUMBO

Serves 4–6
(for a 4–4.5 litre slow cooker)

This tasty seafood stew is delicious served with fresh crusty bread or as a marinara sauce over pasta, topped with a little shaved parmesan.

300g white fish fillets (such as ling, flathead, whiting or
    monkfish)
1 calamari hood, thinly sliced (or extra 100g white fish fillet)
1 onion, diced
4 cloves garlic, crushed
1 red capsicum, deseeded and diced
3 rounded tablespoons tomato paste
1 tablespoon tomato sauce (ketchup)
2 teaspoons Worcestershire sauce
3 teaspoons sweet chilli sauce
3 teaspoons chutney (any sort)
1½ tablespoons chopped fresh basil
½ teaspoon salt
½ teaspoon brown sugar
1 teaspoon vegetable, chicken or fish stock powder
3 teaspoons chopped thyme
1 cup diced canned or fresh tomatoes
1 tablespoon chopped parsley
300g uncooked medium-sized prawns, peeled and deveined
250g scallops, cleaned
pasta, to serve (any sort)
½ cup shaved or grated parmesan cheese, to serve
    (optional)

Cut the fish into 2cm cubes and place in the slow cooker with the calamari, onion, garlic, capsicum, tomato paste, sauces, chutney, basil, salt, sugar, stock powder, thyme and tomatoes. Stir to combine, cover with the lid and cook for 3 hours on Low.

Stir in the parsley, prawns and scallops and cook for 10 minutes more on Low until just cooked through. Add salt and pepper to taste.

Serve over pasta with a little shaved or grated parmesan, if liked.

SALMON, LEEK AND ASPARAGUS COBBLER

Serves 6
(for a 3.5–4.5 litre slow cooker)

150g asparagus stalks
2 leeks, white part only, sliced (or 2 small onions, thinly
    sliced)
700g salmon fillets, cut into 2cm cubes
¾ cup chicken or fish stock (or ¾ cup water with
    ½ teaspoon stock powder)
juice of 1 lemon
½ teaspoon finely grated lemon rind
½ teaspoon Dijon mustard
¼ teaspoon salt
½ cup cream
2 teaspoons cornflour
2 egg yolks
½ cup grated tasty cheese
white pepper, to taste

Cobbler Topping
1 cup self-raising flour
45g butter, melted
1 egg, lightly beaten
1 tablespoon grated parmesan cheese
3 teaspoons snipped chives
3 teaspoons chopped parsley
⅓ cup milk

Peel any tough outer layer of asparagus stalks and cut the stalks into 1cm pieces.

Place the leek and asparagus in the base of the slow cooker and place the salmon on top.

Mix together the stock, lemon juice and rind, mustard and salt and pour over the salmon.

Place the lid on the cooker and cook for 2 hours on Low.

Turn the cooker to High. In a bowl, whisk together the cream and cornflour until just combined, then whisk in the egg yolks. Stir into the mixture in the slow cooker, together with the grated cheese. Add salt and white pepper to taste. Place the lid on the cooker.

To make the cobbler topping, mix the flour, butter, egg, parmesan, chives, parsley and milk in a bowl and drop dessertspoonfuls over the salmon mixture. Cover with the lid and cook for 25 minutes on High.

Serve with fresh seasonal vegetables or a green salad.

MIDDLE EASTERN SPICED FISH

Serves 4
(for a 3.5 litre slow cooker)

250g tomatoes
600g fish fillets (such as trevalla, monkfish or ling)
1½ teaspoons ground turmeric
2 teaspoons ground cumin
1½ teaspoons ground coriander
½ teaspoon dried chilli flakes
½ teaspoon ground cardamom
½ teaspoon finely grated lemon rind
½ teaspoon brown sugar
¼ teaspoon salt
½ teaspoon finely grated green ginger root
1 tablespoon lemon or lime juice
¼ cup coconut cream

Cut the tomatoes into 6mm slices and place evenly over the base of the slow cooker. Cut the fish into 5cm pieces and place in a bowl. Add the spices, lemon rind, sugar, salt, ginger and lemon or lime juice. Mix well so that the fish is evenly and thoroughly coated. Spoon the entire contents of the bowl evenly over the tomatoes.

Place the lid on the cooker and cook for 2½–3 hours on Low. Stir in the coconut cream, replace the lid and cook for a further 5 minutes.

Serve with couscous made by thoroughly mixing together in a bowl: 1½ cups of couscous, ½ teaspoon of finely grated lemon rind, ¼ teaspoon of chicken or vegetable stock powder and 1½ cups of boiling water. Leave to stand for 5 minutes, then fluff up with a fork and serve.

85

CHICKEN

ASIAN SPICED ROAST CHICKEN

Serves 4–6
(for a 3.5–4.5 litre slow cooker)

1.5kg chicken
3 tablespoons dry or medium-dry sherry
1½ tablespoons honey
2 teaspoons grated green ginger root
1 clove garlic, crushed
1 tablespoon sweet chilli sauce
3 teaspoons vinegar (any sort)
½ teaspoon salt
¼ teaspoon five-spice powder
2 teaspoons cornflour mixed to a paste with 1 tablespoon
   cold water
2 spring onion tops, thinly sliced (optional)
boiled or steamed rice, to serve

Remove the skin from the chicken (don't worry too much about the wings, it's too difficult). Just slip your fingers under the breast skin and work the skin off the flesh. Place the chicken in the slow cooker.

Mix together the sherry, honey, ginger, garlic, sweet chilli sauce, vinegar, salt and five-spice powder. Pour over the chicken.

Place the lid on the cooker and cook for 4 hours on High or 6 hours on Low.

Remove the chicken from the cooker and tip the juices into a small saucepan. Bring to the boil, whisk in the cornflour paste and continue to boil until the sauce has reduced and thickened slightly. Add salt and pepper to taste.

Serve portions of the chicken, drizzled with the sauce and sprinkled with the spring onion, if using, over plain rice.

BUTTER CHICKEN

Serves 4–6
(for a 3.5–4 litre slow cooker)

1 large onion, diced
750g skinless chicken breast or thigh fillets
3 teaspoons ground coriander
4 teaspoons ground cumin
1 teaspoon sweet paprika
¼ teaspoon grated lemon rind
1 tablespoon lemon juice
½ cup Greek-style yoghurt
½ cup coconut milk
1 teaspoon chicken stock powder
1 teaspoon salt
2 teaspoons redcurrant or quince jelly or apricot jam
½ teaspoon ground turmeric
1½ tablespoons tomato sauce (ketchup)
1 tablespoon tomato paste
2 teaspoons sweet chilli sauce

Place the onion in the slow cooker.

Remove all visible fat from the chicken and cut into 1.25cm pieces. Place on top of the onion.

Mix the rest of the ingredients together in a bowl and pour over the chicken. Stir to combine.

Cover with the lid and cook for 3 hours on High or 6 hours on Low.

CHICKEN AND CHORIZO RAGOUT

Serves 4–6
(for a 3.5–4 litre slow cooker)

750g skinless chicken breast fillets
2 onions, diced
200g tomatoes, diced
90g lean bacon, rind removed, diced
1 chorizo, diced
1½ tablespoons tomato paste
1½ tablespoons tomato sauce (ketchup)
1 teaspoon sweet paprika
½ teaspoon salt
2 tablespoons chopped parsley
2 teaspoons cornflour mixed to a paste with 1 tablespoon
    cold water (optional)

Cut the chicken into 2cm cubes and place in the slow cooker with the onion, tomato, bacon, chorizo, tomato paste, tomato sauce, paprika, salt and 1 tablespoon of the parsley.

Place the lid on the cooker and cook for 3 hours on High or 6 hours on Low.

Stir in the remaining parsley and thicken by stirring in some or all of the cornflour paste, if necessary. Add salt and pepper to taste. Replace the lid and cook for a further 10 minutes on High.

Serve with plain boiled or steamed rice and/or seasonal vegetables.

CHICKEN MARENGO WITH BACON

Serves 6
(for a 3.5–4.5 litre slow cooker)

1.5kg chicken
1 onion, diced
125g lean bacon, rind removed, diced
200g mushrooms, sliced
1 sprig fresh thyme or ½ teaspoon dried thyme
3 tablespoons tomato paste
juice of ½ lemon
2 tablespoons dry or medium-dry sherry
3 teaspoons cornflour mixed to a paste with 1 tablespoon
    cold water

Remove the skin from the chicken (don't worry too much about the wings, it's too difficult). Just slip your fingers under the breast skin and work the skin off the flesh.

Place the chicken in the slow cooker. Sprinkle over the onion, bacon, mushrooms and thyme. In a bowl, mix together the tomato paste, lemon juice and sherry. Spoon over the contents of the cooker. Cover with the lid and cook for 4 hours on High or 8 hours on Low.

Remove the chicken from the cooker and leave to stand in a warm place while making the sauce. You can do this in the cooker if the dish has been cooked on High, or if cooked on Low, transfer the sauce to a small saucepan and heat to boiling. Remove any excess fat from the surface with a spoon. Stir some or all of the cornflour paste into the sauce until thickened. Add salt and pepper to taste.

Cut the chicken into portions and serve with the sauce and seasonal vegetables.

CHICKEN BIRYANI

Serves 4
(for a 3.2–3.5 litre slow cooker)

1kg skinless chicken breast fillets
1½ tablespoons grated green ginger root
4 cloves garlic, crushed
1 onion, diced
¼ teaspoon salt
½ teaspoon ground turmeric
1 teaspoon ground coriander
1½ teaspoons ground cumin
½ teaspoon ground cardamom
½ teaspoon ground cinnamon
¾ teaspoon garam masala
½ cup chicken stock (or ½ cup water with ½ teaspoon
    stock powder)
3 teaspoons cornflour mixed to a paste with 2 tablespoons
    cold water (optional)
2 tablespoons chopped coriander

Cut the chicken into 1.25cm cubes and place in the slow cooker with the rest of the ingredients except the cornflour paste and coriander. Stir to combine.

Cover with the lid and cook for 3 hours on High or 6 hours on Low.

If the mixture needs thickening, remove the lid and add the cornflour, stirring thoroughly. Replace the lid and cook for a further 10 minutes on High. Add salt and pepper to taste.

Sprinkle with the chopped coriander and serve over plain boiled or steamed rice.

CHICKEN À LA KING

Serves 4
(for a 3.2–3.5 litre slow cooker)

750g skinless chicken breast fillets
125g mushrooms
1 red capsicum, deseeded
1 small onion, diced
1 tablespoon lemon or lime juice
½ teaspoon sweet paprika
¾ cup chicken stock (or ¾ cup with ½ teaspoon stock
   powder)
2 tablespoons dry or medium-dry sherry
½ teaspoon salt
½ cup cream
3 egg yolks, whisked
white pepper, to taste

Cut the chicken breast into 1cm cubes and place in the slow cooker.

Slice the mushrooms and capsicum into thin strips and place in the slow cooker with the onion. Add the lemon or lime juice, paprika, stock, sherry and salt and stir to combine.

Place the lid on the cooker and cook for 3 hours on High or 5–6 hours on Low.

Remove the lid and stir in the cream and egg yolks. Add salt and white pepper to taste.

Serve the chicken over plain steamed or boiled rice.

EASY CHICKEN, LEEK AND VEGETABLE CURRY

***

Serves 4
(for a 3.5–4.5 litre slow cooker)

You can increase or decrease the amount of curry powder in this recipe according to taste. Curry paste can be substituted for the curry powder. You can also substitute a large diced onion for the leek.

750g skinless chicken breast fillets, diced
2–3 teaspoons curry powder
250g leek, white part only, thinly sliced
1 cooking apple (such as Granny Smith),
    cored and diced
1 large carrot, finely diced
200g cauliflower florets
1 tablespoon soy sauce
2 teaspoons Worcestershire sauce
3 teaspoons chutney (any sort) or tomato sauce (ketchup)
3 teaspoons sweet chilli sauce
2 teaspoons quince, redcurrant jelly or apricot jam
½ cup chicken stock or water
1 teaspoon salt
3 teaspoons cornflour mixed to a paste with
    2 tablespoons cold water
65ml coconut cream

Place all the ingredients except the cornflour paste and coconut cream in the slow cooker. Cover with the lid and cook for 4 hours on High or 8 hours on Low.

Stir in the cornflour paste to thicken, then mix in the coconut cream. Add salt and pepper to taste

Serve the curry over plain boiled or steamed rice.

CORONATION CHICKEN

Serves 4–6
(for a 3.2–4 litre slow cooker)

750g skinless chicken breast fillets
2 onions, finely diced
3 teaspoons curry powder
1 teaspoon Dijon mustard
3 tablespoons white wine
3 teaspoons tomato paste
1 tablespoon sweet chilli sauce
3 teaspoons chutney (any sort)
½ cup chicken stock or water
2 teaspoons cornflour mixed to a paste with 3 teaspoons
   cold water (optional)
1½ tablespoons sour cream (optional)

Cut the chicken into 8mm strips and place in the slow cooker with the onion.

Mix together the curry powder, mustard, wine, tomato paste, sweet chilli sauce, chutney and stock or water. Pour over the chicken and stir to combine.

Cover with the lid and cook for 3 hours on High or 6 hours on Low.

Thicken with the cornflour paste, if needed, then mix in the sour cream, if using. Add salt and pepper to taste.

Serve with plain boiled or steamed rice and salad or seasonal vegetables.

GINGER BARBECUE CHICKEN

Serves 4–6

(for a 3.5–4.5 litre slow cooker)

1.5kg chicken

1 onion, quartered

6 sage leaves (optional)

1 tablespoon grated green ginger root

2 cloves garlic, crushed

1 tablespoon Worcestershire sauce

2 teaspoons chutney (any sort)

1 tablespoon white or cider vinegar

2 teaspoons barbecue sauce

2 teaspoons honey

2 teaspoons Dijon mustard

½ teaspoon salt

3 teaspoons cornflour mixed to a paste with 1 tablespoon
   cold water (optional)

Remove the skin from the chicken (don't worry too much about the wings, it's too difficult). Slip your fingers under the breast skin and work the skin off the flesh.

Place the onion and sage, if using, in the cavity of the chicken. Transfer the chicken to the slow cooker.

Mix together the ginger, garlic, Worcestershire sauce, chutney, vinegar, barbecue sauce, honey, mustard and salt and pour evenly over the chicken.

Place the lid on the cooker and cook for 4 hours on High or 6–7 hours on Low.

Remove the chicken from the cooker and set aside to rest in a warm place. If needed whisk in the cornflour paste. Add salt and pepper to taste. Replace the lid and cook for a further 10 minutes.

Dish up the portions of the chicken and pour over the gravy from cooker. Serve with fresh crusty bread and seasonal vegetables or salad.

COQ AU VIN

Serves 6–8

(for a 4.5 litre slow cooker)

1.5kg chicken drumsticks

12 pickling onions, peeled; or 3 medium onions,
   quartered

180g lean bacon, rind removed, diced

200g mushrooms, sliced

1 cup red wine

2 tablespoons tomato paste

2 teaspoons chutney (any sort)

2 teaspoons redcurrant or quince jelly or brown sugar

2 teaspoons sweet chilli sauce

1½ teaspoons chicken stock powder or ¾ teaspoon salt

3 teaspoons cornflour mixed to a paste with 1 tablespoon
   cold water (optional)

2 tablespoons chopped parsley, to serve (optional)

Remove the skin from the chicken drumsticks.

Place the chicken in the slow cooker with the rest of the ingredients except the cornflour paste and parsley. Stir to combine.

Place the lid on the cooker and cook for 3–4 hours on High or 6–7 hours on Low.

Remove the lid from the cooker, turn to High (if set on Low) and thicken with some or all of the cornflour paste, if necessary. Add salt and pepper to taste.

Sprinkle with the parsley, if liked, and serve with plain steamed or boiled rice or seasonal vegetables.

Hints: *You can use a jointed 1.5kg chicken, or 1.5kg of chicken pieces of your choice instead of drumsticks. You could also buy chicken lovely legs, which have had the skin removed.*

CHICKEN CACCIATORE WITH PARMESAN CRUST

Serves 4–6

(for a 3.5–4.5 litre slow cooker)

750g skinless chicken breast fillets

1 onion, diced

90g lean bacon, rind removed, diced

400g tomatoes, diced

1 red capsicum, deseeded and diced

1½ tablespoons tomato paste

1½ teaspoons chicken stock powder

1 teaspoon brown sugar

2 teaspoons chopped sage

2 teaspoons chopped rosemary

1 bay leaf

3 teaspoons sweet chilli sauce

½ cup white wine

2 teaspoons cornflour mixed to a paste with 3 teaspoons
    cold water (optional)

Crust

1 cup self-raising flour

30g butter, diced

¼ cup grated parmesan cheese

½ teaspoon salt

1 egg

1 tablespoon white wine

1 tablespoon milk

Cut the chicken into 1cm cubes and place in the slow cooker with the onion. Add the bacon, tomato and capsicum to the slow cooker with the tomato paste, stock powder, sugar, sage, rosemary, bay leaf, sweet chilli sauce and wine.

Place the lid on the cooker and cook for 3–4 hours on High or 6–8 hours on Low.

Add salt and pepper to taste. Stir in the cornflour paste, if the mixture needs thickening (turning the cooker to High). Place the lid back on the cooker while preparing the crust.

To make the crust, mix together the flour, butter, parmesan and salt and rub together with the fingertips until the mixture resembles breadcrumbs. Mix in the egg, wine and enough milk to make a soft dough. Roll out on a lightly floured surface to the size of the cooker and lift onto the surface of the cacciatore. Place the lid on the cooker and cook for 30 minutes until the crust is cooked through.

Serve the chicken with seasonal vegetables and/or Peppered Rice with Peas (page 54).

Thai Chicken Curry with Coriander Rice Dumplings

Serves 4
(for a 3.2–3.5 litre slow cooker)

700g skinless chicken breast fillets

1 stalk lemongrass, white part only

2cm piece of green ginger root, peeled and finely grated

3 cloves garlic, crushed

1 onion, diced

2 teaspoons sweet paprika

1 teaspoon ground turmeric

1 tablespoon soy sauce

3 teaspoons fish sauce

2 teaspoons tomato paste

2 teaspoons brown sugar

1 tablespoon sweet chilli sauce

¾ cup coconut milk

3 teaspoons cornflour mixed to a paste with 1 tablespoon
   cold water

Dumplings

2 cups cooked rice

1 egg, lightly beaten

1 cup fresh breadcrumbs

½ teaspoon salt

1 tablespoon finely chopped coriander, Vietnamese mint or
   parsley

Cut the chicken into strips and place in the slow cooker.

Cut the lemongrass in half lengthways and bruise with the blunt side of a knife, then chop finely. Place in the cooker with the rest of the curry ingredients except the cornflour paste and stir to combine.

Place the lid on the cooker and cook for 3 hours on High or 6 hours on Low. Add salt and pepper to taste.

To make the dumplings, mix all the ingredients together and shape into walnut-sized balls.

Place the dumplings on top of the simmering curry, replace the lid and cook for 20 minutes more on High.

Remove the dumplings and set aside. Thicken the curry with some or all of the cornflour paste, if needed.

Serve with steamed Asian greens.

Hint: *This curry can be made without the dumplings, but I prefer to make them. They are a good way to use up leftover rice, add extra flavour and save cooking rice for serving.*

CREAMY PAPRIKA CHICKEN WITH KUMARA

Serves 4–6
(for a 3.2–3.5 litre slow cooker)

750g skinless chicken breast fillets
2 onions, diced
250g kumara, peeled and diced
1½ tablespoons sweet paprika
1 teaspoon sugar
1 bay leaf
2 teaspoons Worcestershire sauce
1 cup diced tomatoes (fresh, canned or bottled)
¼ cup water
1½ tablespoons dry or medium-dry sherry
1 teaspoon salt
1 bay leaf
3 teaspoons cornflour mixed to a paste with 1 tablespoon
    cold water
½ cup sour cream

Cut the chicken into 1.5cm cubes, then place in the slow cooker with the rest of the ingredients except the cornflour paste and sour cream, and stir to combine.

Place the lid on the cooker and cook for 3½–4 hours on High or 7–8 hours on Low.

Remove the lid from the cooker, turn to High (if set on Low) and stir in the cornflour paste to thicken. Cook for 5 minutes with the lid on, then stir in the sour cream. Add salt and pepper to taste.

Serve with pasta, rice or seasonal vegetables.

Greek Chicken Stew with Fetta and Olives

Serves 4–6
(for a 3.2–4.5 litre slow cooker)

850g skinless chicken breast fillets
1 onion
1 red capsicum
¼ cup chopped fresh basil
2 teaspoons apricot jam
3 teaspoons chutney (any sort)
1½ tablespoons tomato paste
400g can diced tomatoes
1½ teaspoons chicken or vegetable stock powder
1 tablespoon sweet paprika
1 tablespoon soy sauce
1 tablespoon tomato sauce (ketchup)
1 teaspoon dried oregano
200g fetta cheese
¾ cup black olives
⅓ cup shredded basil, to serve

Cut the chicken into 2cm cubes and place in the slow cooker. Cut the onion into quarters, then cut each quarter into thin slices. Remove the seeds and core from the capsicum and cut into 1cm cubes. Add the onion and capsicum to the slow cooker with the basil, jam, chutney, tomato paste, tomatoes, stock powder, paprika, sauces and oregano, and stir to combine.

Place the lid on the cooker and cook for 3 hours on High or 6 hours on Low.

Cut 150g of the fetta into 1cm cubes and stir into the mixture, together with the olives. Replace the lid and cook on High for 15 minutes more. Add salt and pepper to taste.

Serve the stew with plain steamed or boiled rice or seasonal vegetables. Crumble the remaining fetta over each serving and top with a little of the shredded basil.

APRICOT CHICKEN WITH HERBED FORCEMEAT BALLS

Serves 6
(for a 4.5 litre slow cooker)

1.5kg chicken, skin removed

Forcemeat Balls

125g good-quality lean sausage mince
½ cup fresh breadcrumbs
2 teaspoons grated onion
¼ teaspoon chopped thyme or sage
½ teaspoon chopped parsley
¼ teaspoon salt
1 teaspoon chutney (any sort)
1 teaspoon soy sauce
1 teaspoon tomato sauce (ketchup)
1 tablespoon chopped dried apricots
1 tablespoon finely chopped pine nuts

Sauce

1 cup apricot nectar
1 teaspoon chicken or vegetable stock powder
2 teaspoons sweet chilli sauce
2 teaspoons soy sauce
2 teaspoons cornflour mixed to a paste with 1 tablespoon
    cold water (optional)

Place the chicken in the slow cooker.

Place all the ingredients for the forcemeat balls in a bowl and mix until very well combined. Shape into walnut-sized balls and place around the chicken.

Mix all the sauce ingredients except the cornflour paste together and pour over the chicken and forcemeat balls.

Place the lid on the cooker and cook for 4 hours on High or 7–8 hours on Low.

Lift the forcemeat balls out of the cooker with a slotted spoon and keep warm. Lift out the chicken, cover with foil and leave to stand for 10 minutes before carving.

Turn the cooker to High (if set on Low) and stir in some or all of the cornflour paste to thicken, if needed. Add salt and pepper to taste. Replace the lid on the cooker and cook for 10 minutes more.

Serve with seasonal vegetables.

CHINESE CHICKEN WITH VEGETABLES

Serves 4
(for a 3.2–3.5 litre slow cooker)

600g skinless chicken breast fillets
1 onion
2 carrots
1 large red capsicum
1 large stalk celery
¼ cup tomato sauce (ketchup)
¼ cup soy sauce
¼ cup white or cider vinegar
1 tablespoon honey
1 tablespoon sweet chilli sauce
1 tablespoon brown sugar
½ teaspoon salt
3 teaspoons cornflour mixed to a paste with
    1½ tablespoons cold water (optional)
1 cup baby English spinach leaves or 2 silverbeet leaves,
    shredded
boiled or steamed rice, to serve

Slice the chicken into thin strips and place in the slow cooker.

Cut the onion in half, then cut into thin strips. Cut the carrots in half crossways, then cut into thin strips. Remove the seeds and core from the capsicum and cut into strips the same size as the carrot strips. Cut celery into thin strips the same size as the carrot strips. Place all the vegetables in the slow cooker with the rest of the ingredients except the cornflour paste and spinach or silverbeet. Stir to combine.

Place the lid on the cooker and cook for 3 hours on High or 6 hours on Low.

If needed, turn the cooker to High and stir in some or all of the cornflour paste to thicken.

Stir in the spinach or silverbeet and cook on HIgh with the lid on for 5 minutes more. Add salt and pepper to taste.

Serve with plain rice.

LAMB

FRUITY LAMB TAGINE

Serves 4–6
(for a 3.5 litre slow cooker)

750g lean diced lamb
60g pitted prunes
60g sultanas
60g diced dried apricots
2 teaspoons ground cumin
2 teaspoons ground coriander
1 teaspoon ground ginger
1 teaspoon ground allspice
1 tablespoon chutney (any sort)
3 teaspoons redcurrant jelly
2 teaspoons curry powder
1 teaspoon salt
½–1 teaspoon dried chilli flakes or 1 tablespoon sweet chilli
    sauce
1 cup chicken stock
3 teaspoons cornflour mixed to a paste with
    1½ tablespoons cold water (optional)
400g can chickpeas, drained and rinsed

Place all the ingredients except the cornflour paste and chickpeas in the slow cooker. Place the lid on the cooker and cook for 4 hours on High or 7–8 hours on Low.

If needed, mix in some or all of the cornflour paste to thicken, stirring while adding it. Then mix in the chickpeas. Add salt and pepper to taste.

Replace the lid on the cooker and cook for 5–10 minutes more on High.

Serve with couscous.

INDIAN SPICED ROAST LAMB

Serves 4–6

(for a 4.5–5.5 litre slow cooker)

Ask your butcher to remove the lamb bone for you.

- 1 leg of lamb, bone and visible fat removed
- 1 clove garlic, crushed
- 2 teaspoons finely grated green ginger root
- ½ teaspoon ground turmeric
- 1 teaspoon ground cumin
- 1 teaspoon ground coriander
- ½ teaspoon garam masala
- ½ teaspoon dried chilli flakes (optional)
- ½ teaspoon brown sugar
- 1 teaspoon salt
- 2 teaspoons lemon juice
- 1 tablespoon soy sauce
- 3 teaspoons cornflour mixed to a paste with 2 tablespoons cold water (optional)

Place the lamb in the slow cooker. Mix the rest of the ingredients together except the cornflour paste and rub all over the surface of the lamb. Place the lid on the cooker and cook for 5–6 hours on High or 10–12 hours on Low until meat is tender.

Remove the lamb from the cooker, cover with foil and leave to rest for 10 minutes before slicing. Meanwhile, if needed, mix some or all of the cornflour paste into the pan juices to thicken slightly. Add salt and pepper to taste. Cook with the lid on for 10 minutes more on High.

Slice the meat and serve with the sauce and seasonal vegetables.

LAMB KORMA

Serves 4–6
(for a 3.2–4.5 litre slow cooker)

750g lean diced lamb

2 onions, diced

3 cloves garlic, crushed

2 teaspoons grated green ginger root

2 long red chillies, deseeded and diced

1 teaspoon ground turmeric

1 teaspoon mustard powder

1 teaspoon ground cumin

½ teaspoon ground coriander

½ teaspoon ground cardamom

¼ teaspoon ground cloves

400g can diced tomatoes

¾ cup coconut milk

1½ teaspoons chicken or vegetable stock powder

3 teaspoons cornflour mixed to a paste with 1 tablespoon
cold water, optional

Place all the ingredients except cornflour paste in the slow cooker and
stir to combine.

Place the lid on the cooker and cook for 4–5 hours on High or 8–9 hours
on Low until meat is tender. Add salt and pepper to taste.

Serve over plain boiled or steamed rice.

LEG OF LAMB CREOLE

Serves 6
(for a 4.5–5.5 litre slow cooker)

Ask your butcher to remove the lamb bone for you.

1 leg of lamb, bone and visible fat removed
1 onion, diced
1 carrot, sliced
1 clove garlic, crushed
½ cup red wine or claret
1½ tablespoons Worcestershire sauce
1½ tablespoons vinegar (any sort)
1 teaspoon redcurrant jelly or brown sugar
2 teaspoons sweet chilli sauce

Gravy
½ teaspoon salt or chicken stock powder
3 teaspoons cornflour mixed to a paste with 2 tablespoons
cold water (optional)

Place the lamb in the slow cooker. Add the onion, carrot and garlic.

Combine the rest of the ingredients in a bowl and pour over the lamb.

Place the lid on the cooker and cook for 5–6 hours on High or 9–10 hours on Low until the lamb is tender.

Remove the lamb to a platter, cover with foil and leave to rest for 15 minutes.

To make the gravy, add the salt or stock powder to the cooker. If needed, stir in the cornflour to thicken slightly. Replace the lid and while the lamb is resting cook for 10 minutes on High to heat and thicken the gravy. Add salt and pepper to taste.

Serve with seasonal vegetables.

LAMB ROGAN JOSH

Serves 4–6
(for a 3.2–4.5 litre slow cooker)

750g lean diced lamb

3 cloves garlic, crushed

2 onions, diced

2 teaspoons grated green ginger root

¼ teaspoon ground cloves

3 teaspoons ground coriander

1 tablespoon ground cumin

1 teaspoon ground cardamom

1 teaspoon ground turmeric

3 teaspoons garam masala

400g can diced tomatoes

1 teaspoon chicken or vegetable stock powder

2 teaspoons cornflour

1 tablespoon tomato paste

2 teaspoons golden syrup

2 teaspoons chutney (any sort)

2 teaspoons Worcestershire sauce

½ teaspoon salt

2 teaspoons tomato sauce (ketchup)

2 teaspoons lemon juice

1 cup plain yoghurt

Place all the ingredients except the yoghurt in the slow cooker and mix well.

Place the lid on the cooker and cook for 4–5 hours on High or 8–10 hours on Low until meat is tender.

Mix in the yoghurt, replace the lid and cook for 10 minutes more on High to heat through. Add salt and pepper to taste.

Serve with plain boiled or steamed rice.

SLOW ROASTED SHOULDER OF LAMB WITH BRAISED VEGETABLES

Serves 6
(for a 4.5–5.5 litre slow cooker)

Ask your butcher to bone out the lamb shoulder and remove any visible fat.

- 1 parsnip
- 2 carrots
- 1 potato
- 2 onions
- 2 teaspoons fish sauce
- 2 teaspoons Worcestershire sauce
- 1 tablespoon tomato sauce (ketchup)
- ½ cup water
- 2 teaspoons instant coffee powder or granules
- 1 shoulder of lamb, bone and visible fat removed
- 2 cloves garlic, crushed
- ½ teaspoon salt
- ¼ teaspoon freshly ground black pepper
- 2 x 10cm sprigs rosemary
- 2 teaspoons cornflour mixed to a paste with 1 tablespoon cold water (optional)

Peel the vegetables and cut into 1cm dice. Place in the slow cooker.

Mix together the sauces, water and coffee, pour over the vegetables and stir to combine. Place the lamb on top and spread on the crushed garlic. Sprinkle with the salt and pepper. Top with the sprigs of rosemary.

Place the lid on the cooker and cook for 5–6 hours on High or 10–12 hours on Low until the meat is very tender.

Remove the meat from the cooker and cover with foil. Set aside to rest for 15–20 minutes.

If needed, mix some or all of the cornflour paste into the cooker to thicken the gravy just slightly. Add salt and pepper to taste.

Cut the meat into 1cm slices and place on the vegetables and gravy that have been spooned onto each plate. Drizzle with a little extra gravy.

Serve with creamy mashed potatoes and seasonal vegetables.

Persian Lamb and Rhubarb Stew

Serves 6
(for a 3.5–4.5 litre slow cooker)

The combination of rhubarb with lamb and the addition of herbs and spices make this stew really, really sumptuous. The rhubarb does not dominate, but rather adds a subtle, sharp fruitiness to the dish.

1kg lean diced lamb

500g rhubarb stalks, diced

1 onion, diced

3 cloves garlic, crushed

2 teaspoons ground allspice

1 teaspoon ground cumin

½ teaspoon ground coriander

½ teaspoon ground cinnamon

¼ teaspoon ground cardamom

3 teaspoons chutney (any sort)

1 tablespoon tomato sauce (ketchup)

5 teaspoons brown sugar

1 tablespoon quince or redcurrant jelly (or extra brown sugar)

2 teaspoons chicken or vegetable stock powder

½ cup water

½ cup chopped parsley

¼ cup chopped mint

3 teaspoons cornflour mixed to a paste with 1 tablespoon cold water (optional)

Combine all the ingredients except the parsley, mint and cornflour paste in the slow cooker and stir.

Place the lid on the cooker and cook for 4–5 hours on High or 8–10 hours on Low until meat is tender.

Stir in half the parsley and all the mint, replace the lid and cook on High for 5 minutes more. Thicken with some or all of the cornflour paste, if needed, and add salt and pepper to taste.

I like this stew best served over couscous. Sprinkle each serving with the remaining chopped parsley.

LANCASHIRE HOTPOT

Serves 6

(for a 4–5 litre slow cooker)

700g potatoes
1kg lean diced lamb
2 onions, diced
300g lean bacon, rind removed, diced
1 cup chicken or vegetable stock (or 1 cup water with
    ¾ teaspoon stock powder)
2 tablespoons chopped parsley, approximately

Peel the potatoes and cut into 1.5cm cubes. Place in the slow cooker with the rest of the ingredients and stir to combine well.

Place the lid on the cooker and cook for 4–5 hours on High or 8–10 hours on Low until meat is tender.

Add salt and pepper to taste.

Sprinkle each serve with the chopped parsley. I love this served with buttered fresh crusty bread.

TSIMMES

Serves 6
(for a 4.5 litre slow cooker)

This unusual dish is a pleasant mix of sweet and sour and fruity, a perfect complement to the lamb.

1 apple
2 carrots
2 parsnips
850g sweet potato
1 onion, diced
1kg lean diced lamb
¾ cup pitted prunes
½ teaspoon ground cinnamon
½ teaspoon ground allspice
¾ cup orange juice
1 bay leaf
1 teaspoon grated green ginger root
1 tablespoon tomato sauce (ketchup)
1 teaspoon chicken stock powder
1½ teaspoons marmalade
1 tablespoon honey
3 teaspoons cornflour mixed to a paste with 1 tablespoon
    cold water

Peel, core and dice the apple. Peel the carrots and parsnips and cut into 8mm slices. Peel the sweet potato and cut into 1cm cubes. Place the vegetables in the slow cooker with the lamb.

Add the rest of the ingredients except the cornflour paste and stir to combine.

Place the lid on the cooker and cook for 5–6 hours on High or 10–11 hours on Low until meat is tender.

Turn the cooker to High (if set on Low) and stir in some or all of the cornflour paste to thicken. Add salt and pepper to taste, replace the lid and cook for 10 minutes more.

Serve with seasonal vegetables or over couscous.

PORK

LENTIL STEW WITH ITALIAN SAUSAGES

Serves 4
(for a 3.2–3.5 litre slow cooker)

750g extra lean Italian sausages (available at most
    supermarkets)
1 cup dried red lentils
2 onions, diced
3 cloves garlic, crushed
400g can diced tomatoes
3 tablespoons chopped basil
¼ cup red wine
2 cups chicken stock (or 2 cups water with 1 ½ teaspoons
    stock powder)
1 teaspoon brown sugar
2 teaspoons sugar
½ teaspoon salt
3 teaspoons chutney (any sort)
crusty bread or couscous, to serve

Cut the sausages into 5cm lengths and place in the slow cooker with the
lentils, onion, garlic, tomatoes, 1 tablespoon of the basil, the wine, stock,
sugars, salt and chutney.

Place the lid on the cooker and cook for 3–4 hours on High or 7 hours
on Low.

Stir the remaining basil into the stew. Add salt and pepper to taste.

Serve with fresh crusty bread or couscous.

CASSOULET

Serves 4–6
(for a 3.5–4.5 litre slow cooker)

800g lean diced pork
500g extra lean pork sausages
125g lean bacon, rind removed, diced
400g can diced tomatoes
2 tablespoons tomato paste
2 tablespoons chopped sage
1 bay leaf
15 pickling onions, peeled or 3 onions, quartered
3 teaspoons Worcestershire sauce
3 teaspoons sweet chilli sauce
2 teaspoons sweet paprika
3 teaspoons redcurrant jelly (or brown sugar)
½ cup water
2 teaspoons chicken or vegetable stock powder
3 teaspoons cornflour mixed to a paste with 1 tablespoon
    cold water (optional)
400g can lima or similar beans, drained and rinsed

Place the pork in the slow cooker. Cut the sausages into 6cm lengths with a sharp knife and place in the cooker with the bacon, tomatoes, tomato paste, sage, bay leaf, onions, sauces, paprika, redcurrant jelly (or sugar), water and stock powder. Stir to combine. Place the lid on the cooker and cook for 4–5 hours on High or 8–9 hours on Low until meat is tender.

If needed, stir in some or all of the cornflour paste to thicken.

Mix the beans into the cassoulet, replace the lid and cook for 10 minutes more on High to heat through. Add salt and pepper to taste.

Chilli Pork with Orange

Serves 4–6

(for a 3.5–4.5 litre slow cooker)

700g lean diced pork
1 onion, diced
1 strip of orange rind
½ cup orange juice
2 teaspoons grated orange rind
1 red capsicum, deseeded and diced
1 tablespoon sweet chilli sauce
3 teaspoons tomato sauce (ketchup)
2 teaspoons soy sauce
1 teaspoon chicken stock powder
1 teaspoon quince or redcurrant jelly or apricot jam
½ cup chicken stock or water
1½ teaspoons white vinegar
½ teaspoon salt

Put all the ingredients in the slow cooker. Place the lid on the cooker and cook for 4 hours on High or 7–8 hours on Low until meat is tender. Add salt and pepper to taste.

Serve with plain boiled or steamed rice.

FRUITY PORK WITH CORIANDER

Serves 4–6

(for a 3.5–4.5 litre slow cooker)

750g lean diced pork

180g dried apricots, diced

60g raisins

2 onions, diced

2 carrots, thinly sliced

1 stalk celery, sliced

2 tablespoons chopped red capsicum

1 teaspoon grated green ginger root

1 tablespoon lemon juice

1½ teaspoons brown sugar

2 teaspoons chutney (any sort)

1½ teaspoons chicken or vegetable stock powder

3 teaspoons sweet chilli sauce

1½ teaspoons Dijon mustard

1 cup dry or medium-dry cider

¼ cup water

2 teaspoons cornflour mixed to a paste with 1 tablespoon
    cold water (optional)

2 tablespoons chopped coriander (optional)

Place the pork, dried apricots, raisins, onion, carrot, celery, capsicum, ginger, lemon juice, sugar, chutney, stock powder, sweet chilli sauce, mustard, cider and water in the slow cooker

Place the lid on the cooker and cook for 4–5 hours on High or 8–9 hours on Low.

If needed, thicken by stirring in some or all of the cornflour paste. Replace the lid on the cooker and cook for 10 minutes more on High. Stir in the coriander, if using. Add salt and pepper to taste.

Serve with plain boiled or steamed rice.

SWEET AND SOUR PORK

Serves 4–6

(for a 3.5–4.5 litre slow cooker)

1kg lean diced pork

2 onions

2 carrots

1 red capsicum

1 green capsicum

420g can pineapple rings in natural juice, drained and juice
reserved

1 tablespoon soy sauce

1 tablespoon tomato sauce (ketchup)

3 teaspoons sweet chilli sauce

1 tablespoon dry or medium-dry sherry

½ cup brown sugar

½ cup white or cider vinegar

1 teaspoon salt

3 teaspoons cornflour mixed to a paste with 1½ tablespoons
cold water (optional)

Place the pork in the slow cooker.

Peel the onions and carrots and cut them into thin strips. Remove the
seeds and cores from the capsicums and cut into strips. Cut the pineapple
into strips also. Place all the stips in the slow cooker with the sauces,
sherry, sugar, vinegar, salt and ½ cup of the reserved pineapple juice.

Place the lid on the cooker and cook for 4 hours on High or 8 hours on Low

If needed, stir in some or all of the cornflour paste to thicken. Add salt
and white pepper to taste. Serve over plain steamed or boiled rice.

ROAST PORK WITH CIDER SAUCE

Serves 6–8
(for a 4.5–6 litre slow cooker)

If you would like to have crackling with your pork, simply remove the rind, place it on two paper towels and sprinkle with a little salt. Cover with two more paper towels and place in the microwave on High for 5 minutes. Now remove and cut the backing fat from the rind. Return the rind to the microwave and continue to cook on High until crisp.

> 3kg leg of pork, approximately
> 200g sweet potato
> 2 carrots
> 1 onion
> 1 parsnip
> 1 clove garlic, crushed
> ½ cup dry or medium-dry cider
> ⅓ cup tomato sauce (ketchup)
> 2 teaspoons quince or redcurrant jelly (or brown sugar)
> ½ teaspoon salt
> 3 teaspoons cornflour mixed to a paste with 1 tablespoon
>   cold water

Remove the rind and all visible fat from the pork.

Peel the vegetables, cut into 1cm dice and place in the slow cooker with the garlic, then place the prepared pork on top.

Mix together the cider and tomato sauce and pour over the pork. Spread the quince or redcurrant jelly over the top and sprinkle with the salt.

Place the lid on the cooker and cook for 5–6 hours on High or 9–11 hours on Low until the pork is very tender.

Remove the pork from the cooker, cover with foil and leave to rest for 20 minutes.

Stir the cornflour paste into the juices in the cooker, replace the lid and cook for 10–15 minutes more on High. Add salt and white pepper to taste.

Slice the pork and serve with the gravy from the slow cooker and seasonal vegetables.

BARBECUE RIBS

Serves 4
(for a 3.5–4.5 litre slow cooker)

This recipe is very handy not only for a family, but also if you are having guests for dinner or a barbecue. The ribs can be cooked to a delicious tenderness all day in the slow cooker, then placed under a grill or on a barbecue hotplate for a few minutes to crisp up before serving.

This amount is enough for four, but it can easily be doubled to serve a crowd.

1 kg pork ribs
3 cloves garlic, crushed
¼ cup tomato sauce (ketchup)
¼ cup barbecue sauce
1 tablespoon Worcestershire sauce
1 tablespoon honey
¾ teaspoon salt
1 teaspoon mustard powder
½ teaspoon dried chilli flakes (optional)

Place the ribs in the slow cooker. Mix the rest of the ingredients together, add to the cooker and stir through well.

Place the lid on the cooker and cook for 4–5 hours on High or 8–9 hours on Low until the pork is tender.

PORK WITH LEMON, LEEK AND MUSTARD SAUCE

Serves 4
(for a 3.2–4.5 litre slow cooker)

1kg lean diced pork
2 leeks, white part only, thinly sliced
1 small onion, diced
2 teaspoons soy sauce
3 rounded teaspoons whole grain mustard
2 teaspoons quince jelly or 1½ teaspoons sugar
1 teaspoon finely grated lemon rind
juice of 1 large lemon
3 teaspoons dry white wine
½ cup chicken stock or water
¾ teaspoon salt
3 teaspoons cornflour mixed to a paste with 1 tablespoon
    cold water (optional)
⅓ cup cream
1 egg yolk
white pepper, to taste

Place all the ingredients except the cornflour paste, cream and egg yolk in the slow cooker and stir to combine. Cover with the lid and cook for 4–5 hours on High or 8–9 hours on Low until meat is tender.

If needed, thicken with some or all of the cornflour paste.

Whisk together the cream and egg yolk and mix through the sauce. Add salt and white pepper to taste.

Serve over plain boiled or steamed rice with seasonal vegetables or a salad.

Old-fashioned Pork Pie

Serves 4–6
(for a 4.5 litre or larger slow cooker)

I put this recipe together after a lively discussion on ABC Radio Tasmania on the subject of pork pies. A listener rang in and related that pork pies were traditionally made for fox hunters to take out on the hunt. The hard pastry, generally just used to enclose the meat, was thrown away and only the pork filling eaten. Whether or not this is the case, I do know the pastry on some pork pies I have tasted is indeed very hard. This seemed a great pity as the pastry is actually very tasty, so I decided to try making a pork pie in the slow cooker, while at the same time baking one in the oven by way of comparison. The slow cooker version was much nicer. The pastry is softer and the herbs in the filling are more pronounced, so the pie was infinitely more delicious.

Making a pork pie is well worth the effort. It is best to prepare the filling first as, if the pastry gets cold, it will not roll out properly.

Keep in mind that a pork pie is to be eaten cold, never hot.

Filling
450g lean pork
60g lean bacon, rind removed, diced
2 teaspoons finely grated onion
1 teaspoon chopped sage
1 teaspoon chopped thyme
½ teaspoon salt
3 scant teaspoons plain flour
1½ cups chicken stock (see page 220 but make with 4 cups
    water not 5 cups) or 1½ cups of bought chicken stock
    plus 3 teaspoons of gelatine

Rich Hot Water Pastry
250g plain flour
¼ teaspoon salt
2½ tablespoons milk
2½ tablespoons water
120g lard, roughly chopped
1 egg yolk
a little lightly beaten eggwhite

For the filling, cut the pork into 1cm dice and mix with the bacon, onion, sage, thyme, salt, flour and 2 tablespoons of the stock. Set aside while making the pastry.

Place an upturned saucer or small rack in the base of the slow cooker and pour in 1 cup of boiling water. Place the lid on the cooker and turn to High.

To make the pastry, place the flour and salt in a bowl and make a well in the centre. Combine the milk, water and lard in a saucepan and heat gently until the lard has melted, then increase the heat and bring to the boil. Pour the milk mixture into the well and mix through the flour together with the egg yolk to make a soft dough.

Grease a 16cm round cake tin, line the base with baking paper and grease again.

Cut one-third from the pastry and set aside. Roll out the remaining pastry on a lightly floured surface until large enough to line the base and side of the tin. Fit in place. Roll out the other piece of pastry large enough to sit over the top.

Spoon the filling evenly into the pastry-lined tin. Brush the edge of the pastry with a little water. Cover with the pastry that has been rolled out for the top. Crimp the edges together well. Cut a 2.5cm round out of the middle and cover with a piece of foil 3cm larger than the top of the tin. Crimp around the edges and tie under the rim with kitchen string to ensure a good seal.

Place the tin in the slow cooker and pour more boiling water around it to come halfway up the side of the tin. Place the lid on the slow cooker and cook for 5–6 hours on High.

Remove the tin from the cooker and leave the pie to cool to lukewarm.

Meanwhile, heat the remaining stock in a saucepan to boiling point and remove from the heat. If using bought chicken stock sprinkle over the gelatine and whisk to dissolve. Cool to lukewarm. If the jelly starts to set, simply reheat gently to lukewarm. Pour the stock mixture carefully, a little at a time, into the hole in the centre of the pie. Refrigerate the pie until the filling is set, preferably overnight.

The next day, run a knife around the edge and turn the pie out of the tin.

This pie is delicious served with a really good pickle, such as green tomato or zucchini pickle or piccalilli.

Hint: *Instead of using chicken stock (and gelatine), you can make your own stock for the pie by using the pork bones and the knuckle from a leg of pork. Dice the meat from the bone for the pie, then simply put the bones and knuckle with herbs, salt, an onion and about 3 cups of water in a slow cooker or in a saucepan. Cook for 4 hours on High or 8 hours on Low. If you are using a saucepan on the stovetop, use 4 cups water and cook for 2 hours, then strain off the liquid. Leave until cold and then lift off the fat (this can be kept in the fridge and used later as lard for roasting potatoes). The liquid will be gelatinous when cold, so reheat it to lukewarm and use it as the stock for pouring into the cooled pie. It will set beautifully.*

PULLED PORK

Serves 6–8
(for a 4.5–5 litre oval slow cooker)

Pulled pork is delicious served hot, and equally or more so the next day in a warm bread roll or in sandwiches.

1.5–2kg leg of pork
½ cup tomato sauce (ketchup)
2 teaspoons brown sugar
½ cup barbecue sauce
2 teaspoons honey
2 teaspoons marmalade
1 tablespoon red wine vinegar
2 tablespoons Dijon mustard
1½ tablespoons sweet chilli sauce
2 tablespoons Worcestershire sauce
1 tablespoon rum (any sort)
3 cloves garlic, crushed
1 teaspoon salt or chicken stock powder
½ teaspoon coffee powder or granules

Remove all visible fat from the pork.

Place all the ingredients in the slow cooker. Cover with the lid and cook for 4–5 hours on High or 8–10 hours on Low until the pork is very tender. Lift out and remove any bones.

Shred the meat with two forks and return to the cooker to cook for 20 minutes more on High. Add salt and pepper to taste.

Serve in warm fresh bread rolls, as a filling in wraps.

BAKED HAM WITH MAPLE, MUSTARD AND MARMALADE GLAZE

Serves 4–6
(for a 4.5 litre slow cooker)

Ham cooked in the slow cooker is absolutely delicious and tender. It is one of the few dishes where the fat is left on the meat. The spiced glaze in this recipe gives a final delectable touch for the mere extra step of placing it in the oven for a few minutes to crisp the outside.

I used my 4.5 litre capacity slow cooker to cook a 2.2kg leg of ham. For a larger ham you will need a correspondingly larger cooker.

Up to 2.2kg leg ham
½ cup maple syrup
3 teaspoons marmalade
3 teaspoons balsamic vinegar
3 teaspoons sherry
3 teaspoons whole grain mustard
6 whole cloves
1 piece star anise

Remove the outer skin from the ham.* Score the fat underneath to form a diamond pattern, being careful not to cut right through to the flesh underneath, then place the ham in the slow cooker. Mix together the rest of the ingredients until well combined, then pour over the meat. Cook for 5–6 hours on High or 10–12 hours on Low.

Remove the ham from the cooker and place in a baking dish. Heat the oven to 200°C.

Strain the sauce from the cooker into a saucepan and bring to a rapid boil. Boil until reduced to about ¾ cup. Spoon over the ham.

Bake the ham for 10 minutes, then spoon the glaze from the bottom of the dish over the ham and cook for a further 5–10 minutes until golden.

Serve hot with seasonal vegetables or cold with salads or as a sandwich filling.

* *To remove the skin from the ham, make a small cut on the outer rim and prise the skin back. If you have any problems doing this, simply use a sharp knife to slice off the thin layer of skin.*

STEAMED PORK BUNS

Makes 6 dumplings
(for a 4–4.5 litre slow cooker)

You will need a wire rack to fit in the base of your slow cooker for this recipe.

For the pastry
1½ cups plain flour
2 teaspoons baking powder
¼ teaspoon salt
30g lard
½ cup warm water
1 teaspoon white vinegar

For the filling
250g pork mince
2 tablespoons bacon, finely diced
1cm piece fresh green ginger root, finely grated
1 clove garlic, crushed
1 spring onion, finely chopped
1 cup finely shredded cabbage
2 teaspoons soy sauce
1 teaspoon barbecue or Hoi Sin sauce
1 teaspoon tomato or apricot chutney
1½ teaspoons oyster sauce
1 egg, lightly beaten
3 teaspoons cornflour
¼ teaspoon salt, optional

First make the pastry. Mix together the flour, baking powder and salt, then rub in the lard with the fingertips until the mixture resembles breadcrumbs. Pour in the combined water and vinegar and mix to make a soft dough, adding a few drops of extra water if necessary. Cover and leave to stand while making the filling.

To make the filling, mix all the ingredients together until well combined.

Pour ½ cup of hot water into the slow cooker and turn on to High. Place a wire rack in the base of the cooker and cut a piece of baking paper to fit over the top of the rack. Place the lid on the cooker and leave to heat while preparing the dumplings.

Divide the dough into 6 even pieces. On a lightly floured surface, roll each piece out to a 14cm diameter circle. Divide the mixture into 6 portions and shape into a ball. Place one ball of filling into the centre of each round of pastry. Brush around edges with a little water and gather up the pastry to form a small parcel around the meat. Press edges together to seal well, then turn over to form neat dumplings with the seam on the underside.

When all the dumplings are prepared, place on the baking paper in the slow cooker. Place lid on cooker and cook on High for 3 hours.

BEEF

BOLOGNESE SAUCE

Serves 6
(for a 3.5–4.5 litre slow cooker)

In this recipe diced beef is used in place of minced meat.

1kg stewing beef (such as gravy beef, chuck or blade
    steak)
60g lean bacon, rind removed, diced
2 onions
1 green or red capsicum, deseeded
125g mushrooms
2 cloves garlic, crushed
3 teaspoons chutney (any sort)
3 teaspoons Worcestershire sauce
2 teaspoons soy sauce
2 teaspoons sweet chilli sauce (optional)
1 teaspoon seedless jam (any sort)
1½ teaspoons brown sugar
2 teaspoons beef or chicken stock powder
2 tablespoons tomato paste
1 sprig rosemary
1 bay leaf
½ teaspoon salt
400g can diced tomatoes
2 teaspoons chopped rosemary
3 teaspoons cornflour mixed to a paste with 1 tablespoon
    cold water
pasta or jacket potatoes, to serve

Remove all visible fat from the meat and cut into small dice (about 6mm). Place in the slow cooker with the bacon.

Peel and dice the onions and dice the capsicum and mushrooms. Place in the cooker with the garlic, chutney, sauces, jam, sugar, stock powder, tomato paste, sprig of rosemary, bay leaf, salt and tomatoes. Stir to combine.

Place the lid on the cooker and cook for 4–5 hours on High or 8–9 hours on Low until meat is tender. Remove the lid, stir in the chopped rosemary and thicken the sauce with the cornflour paste.

Replace the lid on the cooker and cook for 10 minutes more on High. Add salt and pepper and maybe a little extra sugar to taste.

Serve as a pasta sauce or as a topping for jacket potatoes.

Note: *Any leftovers can be used as a pie filling, or spread on split hamburger bun halves, topped with cheese and baked in the oven at 170°C for 10 minutes until the cheese has melted.*

BRAISED BEEF CHEEKS WITH MUSHROOMS

Serves 4
(for a 3.2–4.5 litre slow cooker)

750g beef cheeks
250g mushrooms
1 onion, diced
1 tablespoon tomato paste
1 cup beef stock (or 1 cup water with ¾ teaspoon stock
    powder)
½ teaspoon salt
2 sprigs thyme (optional)
3 teaspoons cornflour mixed to a paste with 1 tablespoon
    cold water (optional)

Remove all visible fat from the beef cheeks and cut the beef into 1.5cm cubes.

Cut the mushrooms into 1cm pieces.

Add the beef and mushrooms to the slow cooker together with the onion, tomato paste, stock, salt and thyme, if using. Stir to combine.

Place the lid on the cooker and cook for 4–6 hours on High or 8–10 hours on Low until the beef is tender.

If necessary, thicken the mixture with some or all of the cornflour paste, replace the lid and cook for 10 minutes on High. Add salt and pepper to taste.

Serve with creamy mashed potatoes and seasonal vegetables.

PULLED BEEF

Serves 6

(for a 3.2–4 litre slow cooker)

1.5–2kg piece of boneless beef (such as topside or blade)

½ cup tomato sauce (ketchup)

1 tablespoon mustard powder

2 tablespoons Worcestershire sauce

3 teaspoons brown sugar

1 teaspoon beef, chicken or vegetable stock powder

1 small onion, grated

¼ teaspoon ground allspice

½ teaspoon dried chilli flakes

¼ cup water

2 scant teaspoons cornflour mixed to a paste with
    1 tablespoon cold water

Remove all visible fat from the meat and place in the slow cooker. In a bowl mix together the rest of the ingredients except the cornflour paste and pour over the top. Place the lid on the cooker and cook for 5–6 hours on High or 11–12 hours on Low until the meat is very tender.

Remove the meat from the slow cooker and shred with forks. Stir the cornflour paste into the liquid in the cooker. Place the lid on the cooker and cook for 10 minutes more on High. Return the shredded meat to the cooker and stir to combine. Add a little hot water or stock if needed to make a tasty moist mixture. Add salt and pepper to taste.

Delicious served hot in crusty bread rolls.

CABBAGE ROLLS

Serves 6
(for a 3.5–4.5 litre slow cooker)

This is a wonderful dish to come home to after a day out. It is a complete meal unto itself, but can be served with steamed seasonal vegetables or fresh crusty chunks of bread to soak up the juices.

Cabbage Rolls
6–8 cabbage leaves
2 rashers lean bacon, rind removed, finely diced
500g beef or pork and veal mince
½ teaspoon salt (optional)
¼ cup short-grain rice
1 onion, grated or finely chopped
½ cup fresh breadcrumbs
1½ teaspoons sweet paprika
1 teaspoon chopped thyme (optional)
2 teaspoons soy sauce
2 teaspoons Worcestershire sauce
1 clove garlic, crushed

Sauce
1 tablespoon tomato paste
½ cup tomato sauce (ketchup)
1 teaspoon chicken stock powder
juice of ½ lemon
2 teaspoons chutney (any sort)
1 tablespoon brown sugar
2 cloves garlic, crushed

½ cup water

½ teaspoon salt

2 teaspoons cornflour mixed to a paste with 1 tablespoon
     cold water (optional)

Remove the tough core from the centre of the cabbage leaves. Bring a saucepan of water to the boil and immerse the cabbage leaves for 3 minutes. Drain while preparing the filling.

Mix together the bacon, mince, salt, rice, onion, breadcrumbs, paprika, thyme, sauces and garlic in a bowl until well combined.

Wrap portions of the meat mixture in the cabbage leaves (you may need to cut them up a bit). Place in the slow cooker.

To make the sauce, mix all the ingredients except the cornflour paste together and pour over the cabbage rolls.

Place the lid on the cooker and cook for 4 hours on High or 7–8 hours on Low.

Remove the rolls to a serving dish and, if needed, whisk some or all of the cornflour paste into the sauce, cook for 10 minutes on High to thicken. Add salt and pepper to taste.

RICH BEEF AND VEGETABLE CASSEROLE

Serves 4–6
(for a 3.2–4.5 litre slow cooker)

750g lean diced beef
1 onion, diced
1 parsnip, sliced
125g mushrooms, sliced
1 green capsicum, deseeded and diced
1 stalk celery, sliced
2 carrots, sliced
1 teaspoon salt
½ cup red wine or port
1 tablespoon tomato paste
1 tablespoon chutney (any sort)
2 teaspoons soy sauce
1 tablespoon Worcestershire sauce
½ cup beef or chicken stock or water
1 tablespoon sweet chilli sauce
2 teaspoons tomato sauce (ketchup)
3 teaspoons cornflour mixed to a paste with 1 tablespoon
    cold water

Place all the ingredients except the cornflour paste in the slow cooker, stir, place the lid on the cooker and cook for 4–5 hours on High or 8–10 hours on Low until meat is tender.

Stir in the cornflour paste, replace the lid and cook for 10 minutes on High to thicken. Add salt and pepper to taste.

Serve with plain boiled or steamed rice or creamy mashed potatoes and seasonal vegetables.

SAUSAGES IN ONION GRAVY

Serves 4–6

(for a 3.2–4.5 litre slow cooker)

1kg extra-lean beef or pork sausages

2 large or 3 medium onions, thinly sliced

1 tablespoon vinegar (any sort)

1½ teaspoons brown sugar

1 tablespoon chutney (any sort)

3 teaspoons Worcestershire sauce

1½ teaspoons mustard powder

½ cup beer (doesn't matter if it's flat)

1½ teaspoons cornflour mixed to a paste with 2 teaspoons
    cold water

Place the sausages and onion in the slow cooker.

Mix together the vinegar, sugar, chutney, Worcestershire sauce, mustard powder and beer. Pour over the sausages and onion and stir to combine.

Place the lid on the cooker and cook for 3 hours on High or 6 hours on Low.

Lift out the sausages and thicken the gravy with some or all of the cornflour paste. Add salt and pepper to taste. Return the sausages to the sauce, replace the lid and cook for 10 minutes more on High.

Serve with creamy mashed potatoes and seasonal vegetables.

SPICY TOMATO MEATBALLS

Serves 4–6
(for a 3.5–4.5 litre slow cooker)

500g can good-quality tomato soup
2 teaspoons sweet chilli sauce
2 teaspoons Worcestershire sauce
1 cup water or chicken stock

Meatballs
350g lean beef mince
350g sausage mince
1 slice of bread, crumbed
2 teaspoons soy sauce
2 teaspoons Worcestershire sauce
2 teaspoons smooth-textured chutney (any sort)
¾ teaspoon salt

Mix the tomato soup, sweet chilli sauce, Worcestershire sauce and water or stock together in the slow cooker.

To make the meatballs, mix all the ingredients together in a bowl until well combined. Shape into walnut-sized balls and place in the cooker, ensuring that the meatballs are covered with the liquid. Spoon the sauce over the top, if necessary.

Place the lid on the cooker and cook for 4 hours on High or 6–8 hours on Low. Add salt and pepper to taste before serving over pasta and/or with seasonal vegetables.

TEX MEX BEEF

Serves 4
(for a 3.5–4 litre slow cooker)

800g beef cheeks (or stewing beef such as chuck, blade,
    shin or gravy beef)
4 cloves garlic, crushed
2 onions, diced
1 tablespoon chutney (any sort)
4 teaspoons ground cumin
½ teaspoon dried oregano
2 teaspoons ground coriander
½ teaspoon ground cinnamon
¼ teaspoon ground cloves
3 teaspoons brown sugar
1 tablespoon tomato sauce (ketchup)
1 tablespoon sweet chilli sauce or 1 long red chilli,
    chopped, or ½ teaspoon dried chilli flakes
2 teaspoons soy sauce
3 teaspoons Worcestershire sauce
¼ cup red wine
½ cup beef stock or water
2 tablespoons tomato paste
1 teaspoon salt
3 teaspoons cornflour mixed to a paste with 1 tablespoon
    cold water (optional)
20g dark chocolate, chopped

Remove all visible fat from the meat and cut into 1.25cm dice. Place in the slow cooker with the rest of the ingredients except the cornflour paste and chocolate and stir to combine.

Place the lid on the cooker and cook for 4 hours on High or 7–8 hours on Low until meat is tender.

If needed, stir in the cornflour paste, replace the lid and cook for 10 minutes more on High. Stir in the chocolate until melted. Add salt and pepper to taste.

Serve with polenta or rice or nachos and a green salad.

CUMBERLAND BEEF

Serves 6
(for a 3.5–4.5 litre slow cooker)

1.5kg roasting beef (such as topside or blade)
juice of 1 lemon
juice of 1 orange
1 tablespoon Dijon mustard
1 tablespoon tomato sauce (ketchup)
2 teaspoons Worcestershire sauce
3 tablespoons Marsala
3 tablespoons redcurrant jelly
1 teaspoon beef stock powder
1 sprig rosemary
3 teaspoons cornflour mixed to a paste with 1 tablespoon
    cold water (optional)

Remove all visible fat from the beef. Place the beef in the slow cooker.

Mix together the rest of the ingredients except the rosemary and cornflour paste and pour over the beef. Place the sprig of rosemary on top. Cover with the lid and cook for 5–6 hours on High or 10–12 hours on Low until the meat is tender.

Remove the beef to a plate, cover with foil and leave to rest for 15 minutes before slicing.

Meanwhile, turn the cooker to High (if set on Low) and stir in the cornflour paste, if needed. Replace the lid and cook for 10 minutes. Add salt and pepper to taste.

Drizzle the sauce from the cooker over the sliced meat and serve with seasonal vegetables.

FRUITY BEEF OLIVES

Serves 6–8
(for a 4.5 litre slow cooker)

I usually make this amount to feed quite a few. By all means halve the quantities and cook it in a 3.2–3.5 litre capacity slow cooker.

850g thinly sliced beef (such as topside or round) (about 8–10 slices)

500g sausage mince

1 onion, grated

½ cup diced dried apricots

1 tablespoon chopped fresh rosemary or 1 teaspoon dried rosemary

½ teaspoon salt

3 teaspoons chutney (any sort)

3 teaspoons soy sauce

3 teaspoons tomato sauce (ketchup), plus ½ cup extra

3 teaspoons Worcestershire sauce

1 cup fresh breadcrumbs (about 2 slices of bread, crumbed)

¼ cup sherry

½ teaspoon mustard powder

½ teaspoon stock powder (any sort)

2 teaspoons white or cider vinegar

2 tablespoons water

3 teaspoons cornflour mixed to a paste with 1 tablespoon cold water

Remove all visible fat from the beef.

Mix together the sausage mince, onion, apricots, rosemary, salt, chutney, soy sauce, tomato sauce, Worcestershire sauce and breadcrumbs.

Lay each slice of beef out flat and spread with the sausage meat filling. Roll up and place, seam side down, in the slow cooker, layering as needed.

Mix together the extra tomato sauce, the sherry, mustard powder, stock powder, vinegar and water and pour over the beef rolls.

Place the lid on the cooker and cook for 4–5 hours on High or 8–10 hours on Low until meat is tender.

Remove the rolls from the cooker with a slotted spoon and keep warm.

Stir the cornflour paste into the sauce, replace the lid and cook for 5–10 minutes more on High until thickened slightly. Add salt and pepper to taste.

Serve with seasonal vegetables.

HONEY SPICED CORNED BEEF WITH HONEY MUSTARD GLAZE

Serves 6–8
(for a 3.5–5 litre slow cooker)

While it is not necessary to pour the glaze over the meat, it adds a whole new dimension of flavour and only takes a few extra minutes. Any leftover corned beef is delicious the next day in sandwiches with pickles.

2kg lean corned silverside
3 tablespoons honey
2 tablespoons balsamic vinegar
1 star anise
10 allspice berries or 1½ teaspoons ground allspice
1 onion, halved
1 tablespoon Worcestershire sauce

Glaze
⅓ cup honey
2 teaspoons soy sauce
1 tablespoon balsamic vinegar
1 teaspoon mustard powder
1 tablespoon brown sugar

Place the meat in the slow cooker and pour in enough water to come three-quarters of the way up the side. Add the honey, vinegar, spices, onion and Worcestershire sauce and stir to combine.

Place the lid on the cooker and cook for 5–6 hours on High or 10–12 hours on Low until meat is tender.

Remove the meat from the cooker and place in a baking dish.

Heat the oven to 180°C.

Mix together all the glaze ingredients and pour over the meat. Place in the oven for 15–20 minutes, basting once or twice with the glaze during cooking.

Remove from the oven and leave to rest for at least 20 minutes before slicing.

Serve with mashed potatoes and seasonal vegetables.

COCKTAIL MEATBALLS

Makes 24 meatballs
(for a 3.5–4.5 litre slow cooker)

These meatballs are handy to have as delicious nibbles for a party. However, they are equally suitable to serve as a main meal with seasonal vegetables.

Meatballs
600g good-quality beef mince

1 onion, grated

1 egg, lightly whisked

1 slice of bread, crumbed

3 teaspoons soy sauce

3 teaspoons Worcestershire sauce

2 teaspoons chutney (any sort), mashed with a fork if
   chunky

½ teaspoon salt

Sauce
½ cup tomato sauce (ketchup)

juice of ½ orange

½ teaspoon salt

1 tablespoon balsamic vinegar

1 tablespoon soy sauce

¼ cup firmly packed brown sugar

1½ teaspoons cornflour mixed to a paste with 1 tablespoon
   cold water (optional)

To make the meatballs, mix together the mince, onion, egg, breadcrumbs, sauces, chutney and salt. Roll into walnut-sized balls and place in the slow cooker.

To make the sauce, mix together the tomato sauce, orange juice, salt, vinegar, soy sauce and sugar.

Spoon the sauce over the meatballs and place the lid on the cooker. Cook for 3½ hours on High or 6–7 hours on Low.

Lift out the meatballs with a slotted spoon. If desired, while the sauce is still hot, thicken it slightly by stirring in some or all of the cornflour paste, replace the lid and cook for 10 minutes on High. Add salt and pepper to taste.

WAKEFIELD STEAK

Serves 4–6

(for a 3.5–4.5 litre slow cooker)

800g lean diced beef

1 onion, diced

1 carrot, diced

1 teaspoon ground ginger

1 teaspoon curry powder

1 teaspoon mustard powder

1 teaspoon ground allspice

2 tablespoons sultanas

1½ tablespoons tomato paste

2 teaspoons chutney (any sort)

1½ tablespoons Worcestershire sauce

1 tablespoon white, cider or balsamic vinegar

2 teaspoons quince or redcurrant jelly or apricot jam

1 cup chicken or beef stock or water

¾ teaspoon salt

3 teaspoons cornflour mixed to a paste with 1 tablespoon
    cold water (optional)

Combine all the ingredients except the cornflour paste in the slow cooker.

Place the lid on the cooker and cook for 4–5 hours on High or 8–9 hours on Low until meat is tender.

Remove the lid and, if needed, thicken the sauce by stirring in some or all of the cornflour paste. Replace the lid and cook for 10 minutes on High.

Add salt and pepper to taste. Serve with plain steamed or boiled rice and/or seasonal vegetables.

MOROCCAN BEEF

Serves 4–6
(for a 3.5–4.5 litre slow cooker)

750g lean diced beef
1 onion, finely chopped
2 cloves garlic, crushed
2 teaspoons finely grated orange rind
1 teaspoon ground turmeric
1½ teaspoons sweet paprika
2 teaspoons ground cumin
1 teaspoon ground coriander
½ teaspoon garam masala
2 teaspoons ground cinnamon
2 teaspoons chutney (any sort)
2 teaspoons quince or redcurrant jelly
1 tablespoon honey
1¼ cups chicken or beef stock (or 1¼ cups water with
   ¾ teaspoon stock powder)
2 teaspoons cornflour mixed to a paste with 1 tablespoon
   cold water (optional)

Place all the ingredients except the cornflour paste in the slow cooker
and stir to combine. Place the lid on the cooker and cook for 4–5 hours
on High or 8–10 hours on Low until meat is tender.

Remove the lid and, if needed, thicken the sauce by stirring in some or all
of the cornflour paste. Replace the lid and cook for 10 minutes on High.
Add salt and pepper to taste.

Serve over plain boiled or steamed rice or couscous.

GLAZED SCOTCH EGG MEATLOAF

Serves 4–6
(for a 4.5 litre slow cooker)

6 eggs
250g carrots
1½ teaspoons chopped thyme
750g beef mince
1 onion, coarsely grated or very finely chopped
1 cup fresh breadcrumbs
1 tablespoon chutney (any sort)
1 teaspoon salt
3 teaspoons barbecue sauce
3 teaspoons Worcestershire sauce
3 teaspoons soy sauce
3 teaspoons tomato sauce (ketchup)

Topping
¼ cup tomato sauce (ketchup)
1 tablespoon sweet chilli sauce
½ cup grated tasty cheese

Place 5 of the eggs in a small saucepan and cover with cold water. Bring to the boil, then immediately reduce the heat and simmer for 4 minutes. Drain and cover with cold water. Leave to stand for 4 minutes, then remove the shells by lightly tapping all around and peeling off. Rinse in cold water to remove any shell that clings and set aside while preparing the meatloaf.

Peel and thinly slice the carrots. Grease the slow cooker then place the carrots on the base and sprinkle with the thyme.

In a large bowl, combine the beef, onion, the remaining egg (lightly whisked), the breadcrumbs, chutney, salt and sauces and mix until well combined.

Place a large piece of plastic wrap on the work surface. Shape the meat mixture into a rectangle approximately 23 x 19cm. Place the boiled eggs end to end along the centre. Using the plastic wrap, roll up the meat Swiss-roll style to enclose the eggs completely and evenly, shaping it into a loaf. Again, using the plastic wrap for support, place the loaf in the slow cooker on top of the carrots, then carefully remove the plastic wrap.

To make the topping, mix together the tomato sauce and sweet chilli sauce and spoon over the top of the meatloaf.

Place the lid on the cooker and cook for 3 hours on High or 6 hours on Low.

Remove the lid from the cooker and sprinkle the grated cheese over the top of the meatloaf. Replace the lid and cook for 5 minutes on High until the cheese has melted.

While still in the cooker, cut the meatloaf into thick slices and lift out of the cooker with a slotted spoon or egg flip.

Serve with seasonal vegetables and tomato sauce (ketchup) or chutney, if desired.

Pineapple Meatballs

Serves 4–6
(for a 4–4.5 litre slow cooker)

Although this sounds very 1970-ish, it is a dish that is always extremely popular with the children of our household – and adults too for that matter. Unless you have a great aversion to pineapple, it is well worth making.

When I make this, I often double the meatball mixture and put half away in the fridge for the next night to make hamburgers.

Meatballs
600g lean beef mince
1 small onion, grated
1 egg
½ cup fresh breadcrumbs
3 teaspoons soy sauce
2 teaspoons Worcestershire sauce
2 teaspoons tomato sauce (ketchup)
2 teaspoons chutney (any sort)
½ teaspoon salt

Sauce
1 red capsicum, deseeded
1 large stalk celery
1 small onion
1 carrot
450g can pineapple pieces in natural juice
1 tablespoon soy sauce
2 tablespoons sugar

2 tablespoons white vinegar

1 teaspoon chicken or vegetable stock powder

2 teaspoons cornflour mixed to a paste with 1 tablespoon
cold water (optional)

boiled or steamed rice, to serve

To make the meatballs, mix all the ingredients together well and set aside.

To make the sauce, cut the capsicum, celery, onion and carrot into thin strips approximately 4cm long and place in the base of the slow cooker. Stir to combine.

Roll the meat mixture into walnut-sized balls and place on top of the vegetables in the cooker.

Drain the pineapple and reserve the juice. Place 1 cup of the pineapple pieces in a bowl, add the reserved juice and the rest of the ingredients except the cornflour paste and mix well. Pour over the meatballs.

Place the lid on the cooker and cook for 4 hours on High or 7–8 hours on Low.

Turn the cooker to High (if set on Low) and lift the meatballs out with a slotted spoon. Keep warm.

If needed, thicken the sauce with some or all of the cornflour paste, stirring through while still hot. Replace the lid and cook for a further 10 minutes on High. Add salt and pepper to taste.

Serve the meatballs over plain rice and drizzle the sauce over the top.

Hint: *The rest of the pineapple can be served with cereal for breakfast, or if you are especially fond of it, all of the pineapple can be used in the sauce.*

VINDALOO WITH MINTED CUCUMBER YOGHURT

Serves 4
(for a 3.2–3.5 litre slow cooker)

Don't be tempted to skip the minted cucumber yoghurt with this recipe
as it complements the rich, spiced meat to perfection.

Vindaloo

900g lean diced beef
4 cloves garlic, crushed
1½ tablespoons grated green ginger root
1 long red chilli, thinly sliced
2 teaspoons ground cumin
1 teaspoon ground turmeric
1 teaspoon mustard powder
1½ teaspoons ground cinnamon
½ teaspoon ground allspice
¾ teaspoon salt
½ teaspoon ground cardamom
2 teaspoons brown sugar
½ cup chicken, beef or vegetable stock (or ½ cup water
    with ¼ teaspoon stock powder)
¼ cup white or cider vinegar
3 teaspoons tomato sauce (ketchup)
2 teaspoons cornflour mixed to a paste with 1 tablespoon
    cold water (optional)

Minted Cucumber Yoghurt
½ Lebanese cucumber
1½ cups Greek-style or plain yoghurt
¼ teaspoon salt
2 teaspoons lemon juice
1½ tablespoons chopped mint

To make the vindaloo, place all the ingredients except the cornflour paste
in the slow cooker. Place the lid on the cooker and cook for 4–5 hours on
High or 8–9 hours on Low until meat is tender.

Turn the cooker to High (if set on Low) and thicken, if needed, with some
or all of the cornflour paste. Replace the lid and cook for a further
10 minutes on High. Add salt and pepper to taste.

To make the minted cucumber yoghurt, remove the seeds from the
cucumber and grate the flesh into a clean tea towel. Gather the tea
towel up around the grated flesh and squeeze to remove the moisture
from the cucumber, then mix with the rest of the ingredients.

Serve the vindaloo with the minted cucumber yoghurt and with plain
boiled or steamed rice.

STEAK AND KIDNEY PUDDING

Serves 4
(for a 3.2–4.5 litre slow cooker)

If you don't like kidney, you can simply leave it out, or use some mushrooms instead.

Filling

1 tablespoon vegetable oil
500g lean stewing beef, diced
2 lamb's kidneys, cores removed, diced
1 onion, diced
1 tablespoon plain flour
1 cup beef or chicken stock (or 1 cup water with
   ½ teaspoon stock powder)
2 teaspoons Worcestershire sauce
2 teaspoons chutney (any sort)
1 teaspoon apricot jam
¼ teaspoon salt

Pastry

250g plain flour
125g butter, diced
¼ teaspoon salt
1 egg yolk
¼ cup cold water
1 egg white, lightly beaten

Heat the oil in a large saucepan over high heat and sauté the beef and kidney until well coloured. Add the onion and cook for 2 minutes more. Reduce the heat and stir in the flour, then gradually stir in the stock. Add the Worcestershire sauce, chutney, jam and salt and bring to the boil. Stir until thickened. Add salt and pepper to taste. Leave to cool while making the pastry.

Place the flour, butter and salt in the bowl of a food processor and process until the mixture resembles breadcrumbs. Mix together the egg yolk and water and add to the flour mixture with the motor running until the mixture forms a ball.

Grease a 1 litre pudding basin.

Place a saucer upside down or a low wire rack in the slow cooker and pour in boiling water to a depth of 2cm. Place the lid on the cooker.

On a lightly floured surface, roll out two-thirds of the dough to fit the base and side of the pudding basin. Put the pastry in place and brush, right up to the edge, with a little of the eggwhite.

Roll out the remaining pastry to fit the top of the basin and set aside.

Pour the meat mixture into the pastry-lined basin and top with the other piece of pastry. Crimp the edges together to ensure a good seal. Use any scraps of pastry to make pastry leaves for the top.

Cover the basin with foil and crimp tightly around the edges, then tie with kitchen string. This ensures that no moisture gets into the pudding.

Place the basin in the cooker on the inverted saucer. Pour in extra boiling water to come halfway up the side of the basin. Place the lid on the cooker and cook for 5–6 hours on High or 10–12 hours on Low.

Serve from the basin with seasonal vegetables and creamy mashed potatoes.

SPICED BEEF STRIPS WITH CAPSICUM AND BEANS

Serves 4
(for a 3.5–4.5 litre slow cooker)

1kg lean beef strips
2 red capsicums
1 onion, cut in half lengthways and thinly sliced
2 cloves garlic, crushed
½ cup diced tomatoes (canned or fresh)
1 tablespoon wine (red or white)
2 tablespoons Worcestershire sauce
1 tablespoon balsamic vinegar
1½ tablespoons brown sugar
1 tablespoon tomato paste
1 tablespoon sweet chilli sauce
½ teaspoon salt
1 teaspoon sweet paprika
½ teaspoon ground allspice
½ teaspoon ground oregano
3 teaspoons cornflour mixed to a paste with 1 tablespoon
    cold water (optional)

Place the beef in the slow cooker.

Remove the seeds and cores from the capsicums and cut the flesh into strips the same size as the meat. Add to the beef in the cooker along with the onion and garlic.

Mix together the rest of the ingredients except the cornflour paste and stir into the cooker.

Place the lid on the cooker and cook for 4–5 hours on High or 8–10 hours on Low until the meat is tender.

Thicken the sauce, if needed, with some or all of the cornflour paste. Replace the lid and cook for a further 10 minutes on High. Add salt and pepper to taste.

Serve with plain steamed or boiled rice, couscous or creamy mashed potatoes and seasonal vegetables.

Aberdeen Sausage

Serves 6
(for a 3.2–4.5 litre slow cooker)

Aberdeen sausage is often served cold. It can be made with pork and veal or beef mince.

In this recipe the meat makes its own spicy onion gravy as it cooks.

Aberdeen Sausage
2 onions
300g lean beef mince or pork and veal mince
300g lean sausage mince
250g lean bacon, rind removed, finely diced
2 cups fresh breadcrumbs
3 teaspoons soy sauce
3 teaspoons Worcestershire sauce
1 tablespoon tomato sauce (ketchup)
3 teaspoons plum or barbecue sauce
1 egg, lightly beaten
¼ teaspoon salt

Gravy
¼ cup tomato sauce (ketchup)
2 teaspoons white, cider or malt vinegar
2 teaspoons orange juice
2 teaspoons brown sugar
1 tablespoon sweet chilli sauce

Cut one of the onions into quarters, then cut the quarters into thin slices. Place in the base of the slow cooker. Grate the other onion, place in a bowl with the rest of the sausage ingredients and mix until well combined. Shape into a loaf.

Mix together the gravy ingredients and spread half over the onion in the base of the cooker. Place the sausage loaf on top and spread the remaining gravy mixture over.

Place the lid on the cooker and cook for 4 hours on High or 8 hours on Low.

Remove the sausage from the cooker with a slotted spoon and cut into slices. Drizzle on some of the gravy from the cooker, and serve with creamy mashed potatoes and seasonal vegetables.

DESSERTS

BERRIED APPLE PUDDING

Serves 4
(for a 4.5 litre or larger slow cooker)

Pastry

250g plain flour
¼ teaspoon salt
pinch baking powder
60g butter, diced
60g tasty cheese, diced
1 egg, lightly whisked
⅓ cup cold water
1 eggwhite, lightly beaten

Filling

900g cooking apples (such as Granny Smiths)
½ cup sugar
1 tablespoon cornflour
¾ cup berries (such as blueberries, strawberries,
    raspberries or blackberries)

In the base of the slow cooker, place an upturned saucer or low wire rack. Pour in boiling water to a depth of 2cm and turn the cooker to High. Place the lid on the cooker.

To make the pastry, place the flour, salt, baking powder, butter and cheese in the bowl of a food processor and process until the mixture resembles breadcrumbs. With the motor running, pour in the combined egg and water until the mixture comes together to form a ball.

Grease a 1 litre capacity pudding basin.

On a lightly floured surface, roll out two-thirds of the pastry to form a circle large enough to fit the base and side of the basin and put the pastry in place. Brush, right up to the edge, with a little of the eggwhite.

To make the filling, peel, core and cut the apples into 1cm dice and place in a bowl. Mix in the sugar, cornflour and lastly the berries. Spoon into the pastry-lined basin.

Roll the remaining pastry out to form a circle slightly larger than the top of the basin and put in place. Crimp the edges together.

Grease a piece of foil 8cm larger than the top of the basin and place, greased side down, over the basin. Crimp the edges around the rim to seal completely and tie with kitchen string to secure.

Place the pudding on the inverted saucer or wire rack in the cooker and pour in more boiling water until it comes halfway up the side of the basin.

Place the lid on the cooker and cook for 4 hours on High.

Remove the pudding from the cooker and serve with ice-cream or custard.

RICE CUSTARD

Serves 4–6
(for a 3.2–3.5 litre slow cooker)

This rice custard is particularly nice with stewed or bottled fruits. For a simple dessert, ladle into a bowl and top with a spoonful of raspberry jam.

80g long-grain rice
4 cups milk
100g sugar
4 eggs
½ teaspoon vanilla extract
2 teaspoons cornflour mixed to a paste with ¼ cup milk
½ cup cream (optional)
½ teaspoon ground nutmeg (optional)

Spray the slow cooker with cooking oil spray.

Place the rice and milk in the cooker, stir, then cover with the lid and cook for 3–4 hours on Low until the rice is cooked through.

Whisk together the sugar, eggs and vanilla and stir into the cooker together with the cornflour paste. Replace the lid on the cooker and cook for 5 minutes more on Low.

Stir in the cream, if using, and then sprinkle the nutmeg over the top, if desired.

CARAMELISED APPLE PUDDING

Serves 4–6
(for a 3.5–4.5 litre slow cooker)

90g butter
90g brown sugar
500g cooking apples (such as Granny Smiths)

Cake Batter
1 egg
¾ cup sugar
grated rind of 1 lemon
½ cup milk
¼ cup lemon juice
1 cup self-raising flour
½ cup plain flour
60g butter, melted

Melt the butter and sugar together and pour into the cooker. Peel and core the apples and cut into quarters. Place decoratively over the butter and sugar (this will mean layering them up a bit).

To make the cake batter, whisk the egg and sugar together with the lemon rind in a bowl, then whisk in the rest of the ingredients all at once. Pour evenly into the cooker.

Place the lid on the cooker and cook for 3½ hours on Low or until the batter is cooked.

Turn off the cooker, leave to stand for 5 minutes, then invert the pudding onto a serving platter.

Serve with sweetened whipped cream, custard or vanilla ice-cream.

Boozy Baked Apples

Serves 4

(for a 3.5–4.5 litre slow cooker)

4–5 cooking apples (such as Granny Smiths)
1 teaspoon ground cinnamon
2 tablespoons sugar
250g seedless red or green grapes
¾ cup white wine (such as chardonnay or riesling)
1 teaspoon rosewater
3 teaspoons honey
1½ teaspoons butter, diced

Peel and core the apples, then cut a ring around the 'equator' of each apple to a depth of approximately 6mm. This helps to keep the apples in shape. Place in the slow cooker.

Mix the cinnamon and sugar together and sprinkle into the cavities of the apples. Fill the remaining space with the whole grapes. Scatter the rest of the grapes around the apples and pour over the combined white wine and rosewater. Distribute the honey over the top of the apple centres, then dot the pieces of butter on top.

Place the lid on the cooker and cook for 2½–3 hours on High or 5–6 hours on Low until the apples are tender.

Serve with mascarpone, sweetened whipped cream or vanilla ice-cream.

PEARS IN RASPBERRY AND REDCURRANT SAUCE

Serves 4
(for a 3.2–3.5 litre slow cooker)

The juice that gathers during cooking can be poured off and reduced in a saucepan on the stovetop if desired, or serve each pear with the juice as it stands. Any excess juice, strained, makes a truly delightful after-dinner drink similar to mulled wine.

    4 pears
    5cm strip of lemon rind
    juice of ½ lemon
    1 cup fresh or frozen raspberries
    ½ cup sugar
    ½ cup red wine (such as cabernet sauvignon, pinot noir
        or merlot)
    2 tablespoons redcurrant jelly
    pinch of freshly ground black pepper

Peel the pears, leaving the stalks on, and place in the slow cooker with the lemon rind.

Combine the rest of the ingredients and pour over the pears.

Place the lid on the cooker and cook for 2½–3 hours on High or 5–6 hours on Low.

Serve with mascarpone or vanilla ice-cream.

RICH FRUIT PUDDING

Serves 6–8
(for a 3.5–4 litre slow cooker)

This pudding is rich enough to be used as a last-minute Christmas pudding. It is delicious served anytime with custard.

125g butter
375g mixed dried fruit
juice and rind of ½ orange
1 cup sugar
1 teaspoon ground cinnamon
½ teaspoon ground nutmeg
2 teaspoons marmalade
1 teaspoon bicarbonate of soda
½ cup sherry (any sort)
½ cup water
1 apple, cored and coarsely grated
30g dark chocolate, chopped
2 eggs, lightly whisked
1 cup plain flour
1 cup self-raising flour

Spray the inside of the slow cooker with cooking oil spray or grease well.

Place the butter, dried fruit, orange juice and rind, sugar, spices, marmalade, bicarbonate of soda, sherry, water and apple in a large saucepan and bring to the boil, stirring often. Simmer for 1 minute. Stir in the chocolate until melted. Remove from the heat and leave to stand for

10 minutes. Quickly mix in the eggs and flour until well combined, then pour into the cooker.

Place the lid on the cooker and cook for 4–5 hours on Low until the centre of the pudding is firm to touch.

Serve with custard flavoured with a little sherry or brandy.

COMPOTE OF FRUIT

Serves 4—6

(for a 3.2–3.5 litre slow cooker)

This is a handy way to prepare a healthy breakfast. It can be served with cereals and yoghurt. Use a variety of fresh seasonal, canned, bottled and/or dried fruit. The following is an example of what can be used. If you use dried apricots or other dried fruits, you may need to increase the water accordingly (add approximately an extra ½ cup).

The compote can also be served as a dessert, in which case you can add a little liqueur such as Cointreau. With or without liqueur, it matches perfectly with Rice Custard (recipe page 186).

1¼–1½ cups berries or cherries
12 apricot halves (canned or bottled)
½–¾ cup pitted prunes
⅓ cup sugar, approximately (optional)
¾ cup water

Place all the ingredients in the slow cooker and stir to combine. Place the lid on the cooker. Cook on Low overnight or for 5–8 hours. If needed, add sugar to taste.

CHERRY AND BUTTERMILK SPONGE PUDDING

Serves 6
(for a 3.5–4.5 litre slow cooker)

You can use fresh or frozen cherries in this recipe, in which case the stones should be removed and the cherries cooked with ¼ cup water and sweetened to taste.

If buttermilk is difficult to find, substitute ¾ cup skim milk mixed with ¼ cup lemon juice (don't worry if it curdles when combined).

825g can pitted sour cherries
3 teaspoons sugar, approximately
2–3 teaspoons cornflour mixed to a paste with 1 tablespoon
    cold water

Buttermilk Sponge
1 egg
¾ cup sugar
1 cup buttermilk
1½ cups self-raising flour
60g butter, melted

Place the cherries with their juice in a saucepan and bring to the boil. Add the sugar to taste and thicken with some or all of the cornflour paste. Pour into the slow cooker.

To make the buttermilk sponge, whisk the egg and sugar together in a bowl until well combined, then all at once fold in the buttermilk, flour and melted butter with a metal spoon or whisk.

Spoon the buttermilk sponge batter evenly over the cherries.

Place the lid on the cooker and cook for 2 hours on Low until the buttermilk sponge is cooked.

Serve with custard and/or vanilla ice-cream.

Chocolate Self-saucing Pudding

Serves 6–8
(for a 3.5–4.5 litre slow cooker)

1½ cups self-raising flour
¾ cup sugar
3 tablespoons cocoa powder
¾ cup milk
90g butter, melted

Sauce
1¼ cups firmly packed brown sugar
3 tablespoons cocoa powder
90g choc chips or chocolate melts
3½ cups boiling water
vanilla ice-cream, to serve

Grease the slow cooker.

Mix together the flour, sugar, cocoa, milk and butter in a bowl until well combined. Spread evenly into the cooker.

To make the sauce, mix together the sugar and cocoa and sprinkle over the cake batter in the cooker, then sprinkle over the choc chips or chocolate melts. Slowly pour the boiling water evenly over the top.

Place the lid on the cooker and cook for 3½–4 hours on Low.

Serve with ice-cream.

LEMON DELICIOUS

Serves 4
(for a 3.5–4 litre slow cooker)

This lemon dessert is truly delicious. In the slow cooker it performs very well, making a feather-light sponge on top with a lemon curd underneath.

> 90g butter, softened
> 250g caster sugar
> 4 teaspoons grated lemon rind
> 5 eggs, separated
> 60g self-raising flour
> 1 cup milk
> ½ cup lemon juice

Grease the slow cooker.

Beat the butter, sugar, lemon rind and egg yolks together in a bowl, then fold in the flour and combined milk and lemon juice (it doesn't matter if the juice mixture curdles). Fold in the stiffly beaten eggwhites.

Pour the batter into the slow cooker. Place the lid on the cooker and cook for 2 hours on Low until the sponge on top is set.

Serve with vanilla ice-cream.

CRÈME CARAMELS

Serves 4
(for a 3.5 litre or larger slow cooker)

For this recipe it is a good idea to purchase 200ml metal dariole moulds. Four of these will fit comfortably into an oval 3.5 litre capacity slow cooker. If you have a large 8 litre capacity cooker, you could use 200ml ramekins instead, which are broader than metal darioles.

These puddings have just a hint of coconut flavour – however, it can be left out if preferred, in which case replace the coconut cream with cream.

Toffee
125g sugar
⅓ cup water

Custard
1½ cups milk
½ cup cream
½ teaspoon vanilla extract
3 eggs
2 egg yolks
60g sugar
½ cup coconut cream

Grease four 200ml metal dariole moulds or heatproof ramekins.

To make the toffee, place the sugar and water in a small saucepan and bring to the boil, stirring only until the sugar has dissolved. Boil, without stirring, until the mixture turns a caramel colour. Remove from the heat immediately and pour into the base of each mould or ramekin. Set aside.

To make the custard, place the milk, cream and vanilla in a saucepan and bring to the boil, stirring often. Meanwhile whisk together the eggs, egg yolks and sugar until well combined. Gradually whisk in the hot milk mixture, then whisk in the coconut cream. Strain through a sieve into a jug and pour over the toffee in the moulds.

Place the moulds in the slow cooker and pour in enough hot water to come halfway up the sides of the moulds. Place a piece of foil over the top – I just use one piece, folding in the edges. This helps keep moisture dripping from the lid into the custards.

Place the lid on the cooker and cook for 2½–3 hours on Low until the crème caramels are barely set.

Remove the moulds from the cooker and place in the fridge for several hours before turning out onto serving plates.

CHOCOLATE AND ORANGE LIQUEUR POT PUDDINGS (WITH OPTIONAL BLOOD ORANGE ICE-CREAM)

Serves 4
(for a 3.2–4.5 litre slow cooker)

If you don't wish to make the ice-cream, this pudding can be served with sweetened whipped cream or purchased ice-cream. It is also very nice served with ganache, made by boiling 300ml cream, then removing from the heat and stirring in 300g chopped dark chocolate until it has melted. Add a little orange liqueur if liked.

150g dark chocolate, broken into pieces
90g butter, diced
1 tablespoon orange liqueur
3 eggs
1 egg yolk
90g sugar
grated rind of 1 orange
50g plain flour, sifted

Blood Orange Ice-cream (optional)*
600ml pouring or thickened cream
3 egg yolks
120g icing sugar
grated rind of 2 blood oranges
juice of 3 blood oranges

*   *Although this ice-cream is not made in a slow cooker, it is well worth making as it is the perfect complement to the pot puddings.*

Grease four 200–250ml metal dariole moulds.

Place the chocolate and butter in a heatproof bowl over a saucepan of simmering water (do not let the base of the bowl touch the water). Stir occasionally until melted. Stir in the liqueur. Allow to cool slightly.

Meanwhile beat the eggs, egg yolk, sugar and orange rind together in a bowl until thick and creamy. Gradually beat in the chocolate mixture. Fold in the flour.

Pour the pudding mixture into the prepared moulds and place in the slow cooker. Pour boiling water around the moulds until it reaches halfway up the sides.

Tear off a piece of foil large enough to cover all the puddings and grease one side. Place, greased side down, over the puddings, folding in the edges.

Place the lid on the cooker and cook for 1¼ hours on High.

Using oven mitts, remove the puddings from the cooker. Leave to stand for 5 minutes, then turn out onto serving plates.

To make the ice-cream, whip the cream to soft peaks in a bowl. In a separate bowl, beat the egg yolks and icing sugar until thick, then fold in the cream and orange rind and juice. Pour into a bowl and place in the freezer. When half frozen, beat with electric beaters until smooth, then return to the freezer to freeze completely. Alternatively, churn the ice-cream in an ice-cream machine after the first mixing.

Remove the ice-cream from the freezer a few minutes before serving with the puddings.

Note: *If you want to make the blood orange ice-cream, this will need to be done several hours ahead of time or the day before. Although blood oranges are specified here, Seville oranges could also be used, or Navel or Valencia oranges. Blood oranges give better colour, Seville oranges give a delightful bitterness, but other oranges are delicious also.*

CRÈME BRULÉES

Serves 4
(for a 3.2–4.5 litre slow cooker)

½ cup milk
½ cup cream
1 egg
1 egg yolk
¼ teaspoon vanilla extract
5 teaspoons sugar
⅓ cup caster sugar, approximately

To make the custard, heat the milk and cream in a saucepan until just boiling, then remove from the heat. Meanwhile, whisk together the egg, egg yolk, vanilla and sugar. Gradually whisk in the hot milk mixture, then strain through a sieve into a jug.

Grease four 100ml ramekins and pour in the custard. Place the ramekins in the slow cooker and pour warm water around them to come halfway up the sides. Cover with a piece of foil, place the lid on the cooker and cook for 1¼–1½ hours on Low until just set.

Remove the ramekins from the cooker and place in the fridge to cool.

At serving time, sprinkle the tops all over with the caster sugar and caramelise the sugar with a culinary blow torch or place under the grill for a few minutes until the sugar turns to golden toffee.

GINGERBREAD APPLE PUDDING

Serves 6
(for a 3.5–4.5 litre slow cooker)

This pudding can be served straight from the slow cooker or turned out onto a serving platter.

600g cooking apples (such as Granny Smiths)
5 tablespoons golden syrup
60g butter
30g sugar
1 egg
180g self-raising flour
1½ teaspoons ground ginger
½ teaspoon bicarbonate of soda dissolved in ¼ cup cold water

Grease the slow cooker.

Peel and core the apples and cut into 6mm slices.

Place 3 tablespoons of the golden syrup in the base of the cooker and add the apple slices. Stir to mix, then distribute the apple slices evenly over the base.

Combine the remaining golden syrup and the butter in a saucepan over low heat and stir until melted. Remove from the heat and whisk in the sugar. Allow to cool for about 3 minutes, then whisk in the egg and fold in the flour with the ginger. With a metal spoon, stir in the bicarbonate of soda and water mixture until well combined. Pour evenly over the apple.

Place the lid on the cooker and cook for 1 hour on High until the topping is cooked through.

Serve with vanilla ice-cream or custard.

BERRY MERINGUE PUDDING

Serves 6
(for a 3.5–4.5 litre slow cooker)

800g fresh or frozen berries (any sort)
½ cup sugar, approximately
3 teaspoons cornflour mixed to a paste with
    1½ tablespoons cold water
2 eggwhites
1¼ cups caster sugar
1 teaspoon white or cider vinegar
sweetened whipped cream or vanilla ice-cream, to serve

Turn the slow cooker to Low to preheat for about 5 minutes.

Place the berries in a saucepan and bring to the boil. Sweeten with the sugar to taste, then add the cornflour paste, stirring constantly. Pour the berry mixture into the cooker.

Beat the eggwhites with the caster sugar and vinegar in a bowl until firm peaks form. Place heaped tablespoons of the meringue mixture over the berries.

Place the lid on the cooker and cook for 30 minutes on Low until the topping is set.

Serve with whipped cream or ice cream.

DAPPLED APPLE PUDDING

Serves 4–6

(for a 3.2–4 litre slow cooker)

60g butter
60g brown sugar
1 tablespoon golden syrup
300g apples, peeled and cored (such as golden delicious)

Batter

1 egg
60g sugar
½ cup milk
1 cup self-raising flour
60g butter, melted
1 teaspoon grated lemon rind (optional)
½ cup sultanas
300g apples, peeled, cored and diced (such as Granny Smith)

Grease the slow cooker.

Place the butter, sugar and golden syrup in a saucepan over low heat and melt. Meanwhile, cut the apple into 1cm cubes. Stir the apple into the butter mixture. Pour the mixture into the cooker.

To make the batter, whisk the egg and sugar in a bowl until well combined, then all at once fold in the milk, flour, melted butter and lemon rind, if using. Fold in the sultanas and apple.

Spoon the batter evenly over the apple mixture in the cooker.

Place the lid on the cooker and cook for 2 hours on High.

Serve with custard, cream or ice-cream.

Chocolate Pear Rum Pudding

Serves 6
(for a 3.2–3.5 litre slow cooker)

500g pears
1 tablespoon butter, softened
1 tablespoon golden syrup
¼ cup rum (any sort)

Topping
90g butter, chopped
125g dark chocolate, chopped
2 eggs
1 cup sugar
1½ cups self-raising flour
½ cup milk

Grease the slow cooker and turn to High to preheat for a few minutes.

Peel and core the pears and cut in half. Place the pears, cut side down, in the base of the cooker.

Combine the butter, golden syrup and rum in a small saucepan and heat until just boiling. Pour over the pears and stir to combine, then turn the pears to cut side down once more.

To make the topping, melt the butter and chocolate in a saucepan over low heat. Whisk together the eggs and sugar in a bowl, then all at once fold in the flour, milk and chocolate mixture. Pour evenly over the pears.

Place the lid on the cooker and cook for 2½–3 hours on High or until the chocolate topping is set.

Serve with vanilla ice-cream.

SELF-SAUCING STICKY DATE PUDDING

Serves 6
(for a 3.2–3.5 litre slow cooker)

1½ cups self-raising flour
½ cup sugar
1 teaspoon ground cinnamon
1 teaspoon mixed spice
1½ cups chopped pitted dates
¾ cup milk
1 cup firmly packed brown sugar
1 tablespoon butter, diced
2 cups boiling water
vanilla ice-cream, to serve

Grease the slow cooker.

Mix together the flour, sugar, spices, dates and milk and spoon evenly into the cooker.

Mix together the brown sugar, butter and boiling water in a bowl and pour gently over the date mixture.

Place the lid on the cooker and cook for 2½–3 hours on High until the pudding topping is cooked through.

Serve with ice-cream.

APRICOT CREAM PUDDING

Serves 4

(for a 3.5 litre slow cooker)

825g can apricot halves in natural juice (or equivalent in
    preserved apricot halves), drained
2 eggs
½ cup sugar
¼ cup milk
¼ cup sour cream
3 teaspoons lemon or orange juice
½ cup self-raising flour
½ teaspoon finely grated lemon or orange rind
90g butter, melted
icing sugar, sifted, to dust
vanilla ice-cream or sweetened whipped cream, to serve

Grease the slow cooker.

Arrange the apricot halves, cut side down, over the base of the cooker.

Whisk together the eggs and sugar in a bowl until light and creamy, then
fold in the milk, sour cream, lemon or orange juice, flour, rind and butter.
Pour over the apricots.

Place the lid on the cooker and cook for 2 hours on High.

Dust with a little icing sugar and serve with ice-cream or whipped cream.

BREADS

Breads made in the slow cooker do not brown but on the other hand they are deliciously moist. They are wonderful served with soups or casserole-style dishes as 'gravy soakers'.

FLOWER POT BREADS

🍲

Makes 6 small flowerpot loaves
(a 4.5 litre slow cooker to hold 6 clay pots
6.5cm diameter across the top by 6cm tall)

Guests are always stunned at the novelty of these little flower pot loaves. The flavour of the clay lingers on the bread, which is really delicious.

Unglazed clay pots are necessary for this recipe, but they must first be sealed by deep frying them in cooking oil for 30 minutes at 140°C, after which they are drained and cooled. They only need to be treated once; thereafter, simply spray the insides well with cooking oil or grease them.

For this recipe so that the water doesn't get into the bread through the hole in the base of the pot, roll out 42cm of foil on the bench top and cut into six 14 x 14cm squares. Wrap each piece of foil up and around the base of the pot – it will almost reach up to the rim.

  1 cup plain flour
  1 teaspoons dried yeast
  ½ teaspoon salt
  ¾ teaspoon sugar
  3 teaspoons oil (light olive, peanut or canola)
  ½ cup warm water, approximately
  1 small egg, lightly beaten with 1 tablespoon water
  2 teaspoons poppy or sesame seeds, optional

Mix together the flour, yeast, salt and sugar in a medium bowl. Make a well in the centre and pour in the oil and almost all the water. Mix to a soft dough, adding the rest of the water if necessary and even a little more if needed. Cover the bowl with a tea towel and leave to stand until doubled in size (about 1 hour). Turn out onto a lightly floured surface and knead until smooth and elastic – about 3 minutes.

Divide the dough into 6 pieces and shape each into a ball. Spray the inside of the pots well with cooking oil and place one ball of dough in each. Leave to rise to the top of the pots.

About 10 minutes before the dough has reached the top of the pots, pour ¾ cup of hot water into the base of the slow cooker and turn on to High. Place an upturned flat based plate in the bottom or a small wire rack. Place the lid on cooker.

When the breads have risen, brush them carefully with the egg mixture and sprinkle with poppy or sesame seeds, if using. Place the pots on the plate or rack in the slow cooker, cover with the lid and cook for 2½ hours on High.

Cover with a tea towel, remove from slow cooker and turn out onto a wire rack (you may need to run a knife around the inside so the bread comes out easily).

ANTIPASTO PULL-APART BREAD

🍲,

Serves 4—6

(for a 4 litre [round] or larger [round or oval] slow cooker)

You will need a wire rack or upturned saucer to fit in the base of your slow cooker for this recipe.

1½ cups plain flour
1½ teaspoons dried yeast
¾ teaspoon salt
1 teaspoons sugar
1 tablespoon oil (light olive, canola or peanut)
¾ cup warm water, approximately
¼ cup chopped roasted red capsicum
¼ cup chopped semi-dried tomatoes
¼ cup chopped black olives
¼ cup shredded fresh basil
¼ cup freshly grated parmesan, optional

Mix together the flour, yeast, salt and sugar in a medium bowl. Make a well in the centre and pour in the oil and almost all the water. Mix to a soft dough, adding the rest of the water if necessary and even a little more if needed. Cover the bowl with a tea towel and leave to stand until doubled in size (about 1 hour).

Grease a 16cm round deep sided cake tin and line the base with baking paper, grease again.

Pour 1 cup hot water into the base and turn the slow cooker to High.

Turn the dough out onto a lightly floured surface and knead for about 3 minutes until smooth and elastic. Press out into a rectangle 20 x 30cm approximately and sprinkle evenly with the capsicum, tomatoes, olives and basil. Roll up from the long side (Swiss-roll style), enclosing the filling.

Cut the roll into 5 equal slices and place in the prepared tin, cut side up. Leave to rise almost to the top of the tin. Place the tin on the rack or upturned saucer in the cooker and cook for 2½ hours on High. Sprinkle the cheese over the loaf if liked then, replace the lid and cook for 15 minutes more.

Remove from slow cooker, leave to stand for 5 minutes, then turn out onto a wire rack to cool for 20 minutes at least before serving.

HANDY EXTRAS

FAMILY PORRIDGE

Serves 4
(for a 3.2–3.5 litre slow cooker)

It is absolutely necessary to obtain steel cut oats for this slow-cooked porridge. The regular rolled oats will cook to a horrible sludge. Steel cut oats are available from most health food stores.

If you can get hold of a 1 or 1.5 litre capacity slow cooker, use half the amount specified here for an ideal healthy breakfast for two.

> 1 cup steel cut oats
> 5 cups water
> pinch of salt
> honey and milk, to serve

Place all the ingredients in the slow cooker and stir to combine.

Place the lid on the cooker and cook for 8 hours on Low.

Serve each bowlful with a splash of honey and milk.

GARLIC BREAD

Serves 4
(for a 3.2–3.5 litre slow cooker)

Although garlic bread cooked in the slow cooker will not be crisp, it is deliciously soft and moist. It is also very convenient and saves all the preparation of cooking at the last minute. You can, of course, crisp the bread by removing the foil and placing the bread under a hot grill or in the oven for just a few minutes at the end of cooking time.

If the recipe is doubled, you could easily use a 4.5 litre capacity cooker.

> 2 tablespoons water
> 30cm French bread stick
> 90g butter, softened
> 2 cloves garlic, crushed
> 1 tablespoon chopped parsley

Place the water in the base of the slow cooker.

Cut the bread stick into 2cm slices.

Mix the butter, garlic and parsley in a bowl.

Spread each side of the slices of bread with the garlic butter and join back together. Wrap half the bread in foil and place in the cooker, seam side up. Repeat with the remaining bread.

Place the lid on the cooker and cook for 1 hour on High or 2 hours on Low.

STEAMED RICE

Serves 6–8
(for a 3.2–4.5 litre slow cooker)

2 cups long-grain rice
¼ teaspoon salt
5½ cups warm water

Place all the ingredients in the slow cooker, stir to combine and then cover with the lid and cook for 2 hours on High or 4 hours on Low.

Fluff up the rice with a fork and serve as an accompaniment to savoury dishes.

BEEF STOCK

Makes 1 litre, approximately
(for a 4–5.5 litre slow cooker)

This beautiful stock is so deliciously rich that it usually forms a jelly when it gets cold – a sure sign of its excellent quality.

1kg beef bones, approximately
1 carrot, chopped
1 onion, chopped (no need to peel)
1 small stalk celery or 10 celery leaves, chopped
1 bay leaf
1½ teaspoons salt
1 sprig thyme (optional)
5 cups water

Wash the beef bones and place in the slow cooker with the rest of the ingredients.

Cover the cooker with the lid and cook for 4–6 hours on High or 10–12 hours on Low.

Strain the stock through a sieve and place in the fridge to cool. If you want a clearer stock, line the sieve with muslin.

Next day, remove the fat layer from the stock. It is now ready to use.

Store in the fridge for up to 5 days, or in the freezer for up to 3 months.

CHICKEN STOCK

Makes 1 litre, approximately
(for a 4–5 litre slow cooker)

2 chicken carcasses or 500g chicken wings, necks or the
    carcass and trimmings from a roasted chicken
1 carrot, chopped
1 onion, chopped
1 small stalk celery or 10 celery leaves, chopped
1 bay leaf
1½ teaspoons salt
1 sprig thyme (optional)
5 cups water

Wash the chicken bones and place in the slow cooker with the rest of
the ingredients.

Cover the cooker with the lid and cook for 4–6 hours on High or
10–12 hours on Low.

Strain the stock through a sieve and place in the fridge to cool.

Next day, remove the fat layer from the stock. It is now ready to use.

Store in the fridge for up to 4 days, or in the freezer for up to 3 months.

VEGETABLE STOCK

Makes 1 litre, approximately
(for a 4–5.5 litre slow cooker)

You can use virtually any vegetables or vegetable scraps to make this stock. If you are aiming for colour, include some well-washed onion skins. Be careful of using vegetables with an overpowering flavour, such as swedes and turnips.

It is best to leave out potatoes as they will make the stock cloudy.

    5 cups of a range of chopped vegetables or scrubbed
        vegetable skins
    1 onion, chopped
    1 sprig thyme
    1 bay leaf
    1 teaspoon salt
    5 cups water

Place the vegetables or peelings in the slow cooker with the rest of the ingredients.

Cover the cooker with the lid and cook for 4–6 hours on High or 10–12 hours on Low.

Strain the stock through a sieve, add salt to taste if desired and place in the fridge to cool. Store in the fridge for up to 4 days, or in the freezer for up to 6 months.

PRESERVES

I love making the most of a summer's abundance of fruit so I was delighted recently when I discovered that the slow cooker can be a great asset for preserving. I found that the preserves made in the slow cooker have slightly different characteristics to those made on the stovetop; for instance the flavours are slightly stronger and pleasingly sharper.

The slow cooker is perfect for softening the fruit for jam or marmalade and this slow cooking process seems to help in extracting maximum pectin, which means the jam will set well and more quickly. It is best to use fruits that do not oxidise, such as berries or dark plums. However, you can combine fruits that tend to go brown when exposed to air, such as nectarines and peaches, with non-oxidising fruit, such as raspberries, to make jams such as the delicious peach and raspberry jam in this section.

When the fruit is soft, transfer it to a large saucepan on the stovetop, add the sugar and boil for 20–30 minutes until setting point is reached.

Savoury preserves such as chutney and relishes can be made entirely in the slow cooker. They just need a little extra thickening at the end.

Setting point and sterilising jars and bottles

To know when you have reached setting point, place 2 teaspoons of the hot mixture on a cold saucer, place in the fridge for a few minutes. Run your finger through the cold jam; if the surface is quite firm and wrinkles when you pull your finger through it, the jam has reached setting point.

To sterilise the jars, wash in hot soapy water, rinse and place upside down on a clean cloth or dish drainer to drain. Place on a tray in a cold oven. Turn the oven to 110°C (fan forced) or 130°C (not fan forced). When the oven reaches this temperature, turn off the heat and leave the bottles for 10 minutes. To make sure the lids are sterile, thoroughly wash and dry them. When the lid is placed on the jar of hot jelly, turn the jar briefly upside down – the heat of the jelly will sterilise the lid.

PEACH AND RASPBERRY JAM

Makes approximately 1.1 litres
(for a 3.2–3.5 litre slow cooker)

You will need about 650g peaches for this recipe as 500g of peach flesh is needed. You can double the quantities in this recipe if you have a larger cooker.

500g sliced or diced peach flesh, chopped
500g fresh or (thawed) frozen raspberries
1kg sugar

Place the raspberries and peaches in the slow cooker and stir to combine. Place lid on cooker and cook on Low for 5 hours until the peaches are soft.

Allow to cool slightly (for ease of handling), then transfer the mixture to a large saucepan. Bring to the boil, then stir in the sugar. Bring back to the boil, stirring until the sugar is dissolved, then boil over medium heat until setting point is reached (see page 224).

Pour into warm sterilised jars (see page 224) and seal immediately.

Store in a very cool, dry, dark place or in the fridge. Refrigerate after opening.

BERRY JELLY

Makes approximately 900ml
(for a 3.2–3.5 litre slow cooker)

This jelly is delicious served on scones, fresh bread, pikelets or toast. It can be melted as needed and used as a glaze over berry tarts. Add ½ teaspoon to a cup of gravy for a lovely subtle fruitiness or add I teaspoon to a casserole-style dish.

1kg fresh or (thawed) frozen berries
juice 1 lemon
1 cup water
sugar

Place the berries, lemon juice and water in the slow cooker. Place the lid on the cooker and cook on Low for 5 hours. Leave until cool enough to handle, then strain though a fine sieve, pressing the berries down to break them up to extract maximum liquid. Strain the resulting juice through a sieve lined with a single layer of muslin (or even a thin cloth).

Measure the resulting liquid and place in a large saucepan. Add 1 cup of sugar for each cup of juice and bring to the boil, stirring. Boil until setting point is reached (see page 224). Pour into warm sterilised jars and seal immediately (see page 224).

Store in a very cool, dry, dark place or in the fridge. Refrigerate after opening.

MARMALADE

Makes approximately 1.4 litres
(for a 3.5–5 litre slow cooker)

The peel softened in the slow cooker leads to a delicious tart marmalade, much like Seville orange marmalade, with the convenience of being able to make it any time of the year using any type of orange. I like to cut the fruit by hand for this recipe – it leads to a lovely, somewhat chunky, texture.

500g oranges
1 lemon
5 cups water
1.5kg sugar

Finley slice or chop the oranges and lemons and place in the slow cooker with the water. Place the lid on the cooker and cook on Low for 5–6 hours until the skins are soft. When the cooker is cool enough to handle, pour the contents into a large pot and add the sugar. Bring to the boil, stirring until the sugar is dissolved.

Boil for 20–25 minutes over medium heat until setting point is reached (see page 224). Pour into warm sterilised jars and seal immediately (see page 224).

Store in a very cool, dry, dark place or in the fridge. Refrigerate after opening.

PLUM OR BERRY SYRUP

Makes approximately 1.5 litres
(for a 3.5 –4.5 litre slow cooker)

You can use any type of plums to make this syrup. I like the dark skins and flesh of blood plums which make the colour of the finished syrup sensational and the flavour intense.

It can be served as a cordial, mixing one part syrup with 4 parts chilled water, soda water or lemonade. It is also delicious served over ice cream or panna cotta.

> 1kg blood or Japanese plums or berries
> 3 cups water
> sugar
> 2 level teaspoons citric or tartaric acid

Place the plums or berries and water in the slow cooker with the water. Cover with the lid and cook for 8 hours on Low.

Pour the mixture through a sieve (without pressing any of the pulp through), and if a really clear syrup is desired, pour the resulting liquid through another sieve lined with muslin or fine cloth.

Pour into a large saucepan. For each cup of the resulting liquid add 1 cup of sugar. Bring to the boil, stirring to dissolve the sugar and simmer for two minutes only. Stir in the citric acid. Pour into warm sterilised bottles and seal immediately (see page 224).

Store in the fridge or in a very cool, dry, dark place. Refrigerate after opening.

TOMATO RELISH

Makes approximately 1 litre
(for a 3.5 to 4.5 litre slow cooker)

You can peel the tomatoes for this recipe if you like but I never do. If you choose to do so, plunge the whole tomatoes into boiling water for a few seconds, then into iced water, after which the skins should slip off easily.

This recipe can also be used as a tomato sauce (ketchup) by simply puréeing the mixture at the end of the process with a stick blender. In this case use one teaspoon less of the cornflour.

1kg ripe tomatoes
250g onions
1 cooking apple (such as Granny Smith or Golden
    Delicious), cored and grated
250g sugar
1½ teaspoons curry powder
1½ teaspoons mustard powder
1 tablespoon salt
1¼ cups white vinegar
6 teaspoons cornflour mixed to a paste with
    1½ tablespoons white vinegar

Dice the tomatoes and onions and place in the slow cooker with the rest of the ingredients, except the cornflour paste. Place the lid on the cooker and cook on High for 6 hours. Stir in the cornflour paste, cover with the lid and cook for 10 minutes more.

Pour into warm sterilised bottles (see page 224) and seal immediately.

Store in a very cool, dry, dark place or in the fridge. Refrigerate after opening.

Quince Cheese

(for a 3.2–3.5 litre slow cooker)

unblemished quinces (however many your slow cooker will
hold)
¾ cup water
sugar

Rub the quinces with a dry cloth to remove any remaining furry 'bloom'.
Place the whole quinces into the slow cooker and pour over the water.
Place the lid on the cooker and cook on Low for 8–10 hours or until very
soft. Leave to cool, then cut the flesh (including the skin) from the core
and press through a sieve or food mill. For each cup of the resulting
purée, add 1 cup of sugar. Place in a large pot and bring to the boil
stirring constantly. Reduce heat and cook over low heat, stirring almost
constantly with a wooden spoon until the stage when the spoon is
dragged through the middle of the mixture it leaves a clear trail to the
base of the pan.*

Line a square or rectangular tin with foil and pour mixture in (the size of
the tin will depend on the amount of mixture – the cheese should be
about 1.25cm thick). Leave to set, then cut into squares to serve as part
of a cheese platter. Small squares are also very nice coated in chocolate
for a special sweet treat, or even simply rolled in castor sugar.

* *If you tire of stirring before the mixture reaches this 'cheese' stage, simply
pour the mixture into small wide-mouthed containers, in which case it is
technically quince paste which can also be served as part of a cheese platter.*

INDEX

231

ABOUT THE AUTHOR

Sally Wise is a regular guest on ABC Local Radio 936 Hobart, as well as ABC Capricornia with Georgia Stynes. She regularly does presentations for *Sustainable Living*, Melbourne Food and Wine Festival (Masterclasses, 2011), The Agrarian Kitchen Farm Cooking School, The Essential Ingredient (Melbourne, 2011) and various community groups. Sally conducts vocational and training classes where she especially promotes the skill of food preserving to high school home economics teachers. Preserving is now a part of the Victorian home economics curriculum.

She makes and sells her cakes and preserves at a local café as well as at her own 'farm gate stall', and, if time permits, she caters for local functions.

In October 2011, the *Weekend Australian* listed Sally as sixth top cookbook writer in Australia just one below Jamie Oliver.

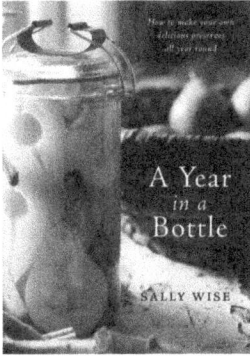

A YEAR IN A BOTTLE

More than a 100 mouthwatering recipes for making your own preserves and conserves. From luscious jellies and jams to delicious pickles and chutneys, this inspiring and practical book makes preserving easy and fun.

It now includes a fruit chart for apricots, apples and pears showing which varieties are best for different methods of preserving.

SLOW COOKER

Easy, nutritious and yummy, slow cooking is ideal for people who are time poor but want to eat healthily. This first volume of slow cooking recipes has been drawn from Sally's collection, developed over 30 years of preparing delicious, economical and healthy meals for her family.

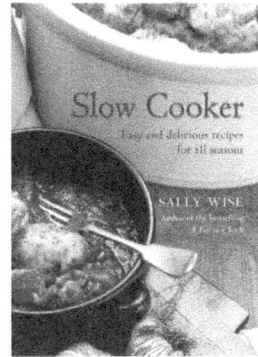

OUT OF THE BOTTLE

Contains tips and basic methods for the novice preserver as well as a collection of Sally's favourite preserving recipes. There are lots of scrumptious recipes in which the preserves are used — from stir-fries to roasts, curries, vegetables dishes and savoury tarts; from mini cherry mud cakes to hummingbird muffins — all focusing on flavour, quick and easy preparation and natural ingredients.

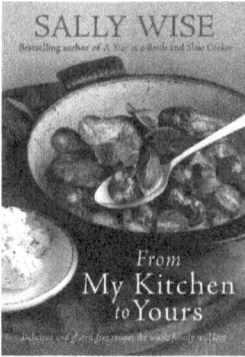

FROM MY KITCHEN TO YOURS

Endorsed by the Coeliac Society of Australia
Over 170 gluten-free recipes

Here are Sally's top recipes for the gluten intolerant. Sally shares her secrets for making food that tastes so good you'll never know you're eating gluten free. As a bonus, there are tips throughout for dairy-free substitutions.

LEFTOVER MAKEOVERS

Sally shows how to turn almost any kind of leftover into a new and delicious meal, snack or sweet treat. From bread to fruit to cooked meat and vegetables, rice and pasta and even scrapings from jam and peanut butter jars, there is a simple, scrumptious and economical way to transform what you've already got into tonight's dinner.

SWEET!

Packed full of delectable, heavenly recipes for the person with a sweet tooth, it includes not only cakes, biscuits and desserts but a section on making your own confectionary. There are even recipes for those who need to watch their sugar intake.